T0067798

The Hawthorne
Community

Emergence and Survival of a Historic
Indianapolis Neighborhood

Charles Guthrie and Diane Arnold

authorHOUSE®

AuthorHouse™
1663 Liberty Drive
Bloomington, IN 47403
www.authorhouse.com
Phone: 833-262-8899

© 2022 Charles Guthrie and Diane Arnold. All rights reserved.

No part of this book may be reproduced, stored in a retrieval system, or
transmitted by any means without the written permission of the author.

Published by AuthorHouse 10/27/2022

ISBN: 978-1-6655-7277-4 (sc)
ISBN: 978-1-6655-7278-1 (e)

Print information available on the last page.

Any people depicted in stock imagery provided by Getty Images are models,
and such images are being used for illustrative purposes only.
Certain stock imagery © Getty Images.

This book is printed on acid-free paper.

Because of the dynamic nature of the Internet, any web addresses or links contained in
this book may have changed since publication and may no longer be valid. The views
expressed in this work are solely those of the author and do not necessarily reflect the
views of the publisher, and the publisher hereby disclaims any responsibility for them.

Dedicated to Hawthorne Neighborhood Leaders
whose service to residents over many years
reflects a deep commitment to community.

Contents

Figures

CHAPTER 1

Introduction: What's in a Name?

If you drive west on Washington Street from downtown Indianapolis, cross the White River and pass the Indianapolis Zoo, you are in the neighborhood of Stringtown. If you continue on for a few more blocks and cross Belmont Avenue you are in the Hawthorne neighborhood. The name Hawthorne is familiar to many these days. But Hawthorne *as a historic neighborhood* is not so well known in the city, and in recent years people are confused by other popular names associated with it. For instance, the public frequently speaks about the "Nearwestside Neighborhood" without realizing this is a fairly recent umbrella term of convenience, but a misleading term that describes an area encompassing three very different historic residential neighborhoods: Haughville, Stringtown, and Hawthorne. The reference to West Washington Street is also sometimes used to refer very generally to that same area, without understanding exactly what it includes. Or, a few years ago you might have heard a popular reference to "Little Mexico" because of the visible influx of Mexican-Americans and their businesses into this area that began in the 1980s and 1990s.

Those involved with any of the city's Westside social services or neighborhood redevelopment projects in recent years, or with George Washington High School, will be familiar with the name *Hawthorne*. For they likely came in contact with the historic and long active Hawthorne Community Center. But they, too, are unlikely to know about Hawthorne as a clearly defined

1

neighborhood with a distinctive history similar to Haughville to its north, or Stringtown to its east.

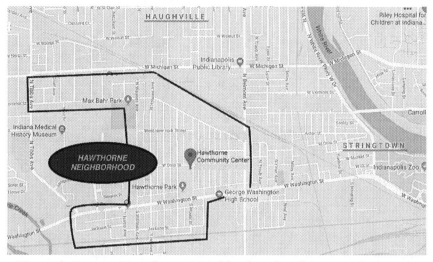

Figure 1 Current Hawthorne Neighborhood and Surrounding Area

background map courtesy of Google Maps

Those who know a bit more about the history of this area might ask, "A long time ago wasn't that Mt. Jackson?" Or, "Wasn't that once part of Haughville?" The answer to both of those questions is a qualified "Well, yes and no." The history is complicated. Mt. Jackson was a small rural village that emerged in the early 19th century along the old National Road just east of Little Eagle Creek a couple of miles from Indianapolis. By the time it incorporated in 1889, the village had grown very little and was still surrounded by farmland (See fig. 2). When the rapidly developing town of Haughville to its north had incorporated in 1883, even though its residential and business construction services extended south to West Michigan Street (effectively down to the railroad), its incorporation boundaries were drawn to include that unoccupied but privately owned farmland to its south down to the National Road (Washington Street).

In the early 20th century that same strip of farmland was sold and sprouted a fast developing residential area that became well known in the life of the city, particularly after World War I. This activity was not associated with Haughville in any way except that it had been included on the original map of incorporation. Neither Mt. Jackson, south of Washington Street, nor Haughville from West Michigan Street north ever made any effort to impose its control over that emerging suburb in between. So it was left to evolve into an independent residential neighborhood that eventually became known as "Hawthorne."

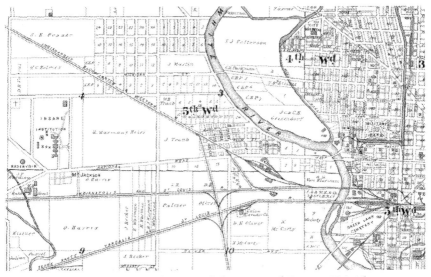

Figure 2 Early Mt Jackson and the Area of Future Hawthorne

Indiana Historical Society, detail from Durant 1876 Map

Haughville has a major entry and numerous references in the very thorough and impressive *Encyclopedia of Indianapolis* (1994).[1] Stringtown neighborhood, on Hawthorne's east side, likewise has an entry and other references in this work. The *Encyclopedia* also includes Stringtown and Haughville on its long list of "Places and Localities" (which includes "Towns, Communities, and Neighborhoods") in Indianapolis. But it does not include any such reference to Hawthorne, or even to the much older frontier village of Mount Jackson which is clearly marked on the early city maps. In other words, even though by the time that the *Encyclopedia of Indianapolis* was published Hawthorne had been a viable and distinctive neighborhood with clearly recognized boundaries and fully integrated into the city's activities and news for decades, it was not included in this important history of Indianapolis.

Wikipedia, for instance, drawing upon this important encyclopedic resource did not include Hawthorne on its list of Indianapolis neighborhoods as it entered the early years of the twenty-first century, even though Hawthorne's immediate neighbors are included. This was certainly surprising to those residents who had long identified themselves as "from Hawthorne Neighborhood." This neighborhood has produced fond memories for generations of folk who took great pride in their community and who knew exactly where the boundaries were that separated them from their neighbors: Vermont and Turner Streets in the north just south of the railroad tracks, south of Washington Street down to the railroad tracks, Belmont Avenue in the east, and Tibbs Avenue in the west.

Hawthorne is not alone in its absence from the popular historical record in this part of the city. There are names used in this area for generations to designate a place with clear informal boundaries known and respected by surrounding neighborhoods, but without having achieved any kind of permanent official recognition. Some community names have disappeared from the public's memory completely, such as *Indianola*, a very early settlement that once existed at the western edge of the White River (now part of Stringtown). All that remains of that settlement now is a trace in the name of a small neighborhood park. Older residents on the Westside have clung to other names that have faded in the minds of outsiders, names that residents once (and still) called home, names that were used to distinguish themselves from their neighbors: *The Valley, The Hill, The Hollow*. Hawthorne has survived this public failure, though barely.

Although Hawthorne's role in more recent developments on the Westside has awakened a greater awareness of the name, particularly because of the work of the Hawthorne Community Center, its full history remains untold. It is time to enter the story of this historic neighborhood clearly into the public record. The story begins on Indiana's early frontier.

CHAPTER 2

Mt. Jackson: "The City's First Suburb"

When the city of Indianapolis was laid out in 1821, early maps indicate that a few settlers had already crossed the White River and staked out claims along the west bank, with a smattering of claims along a rough westward track. There was no sustained traffic in that direction until after 1833 when construction of the great National Road (US 40), extending from Maryland into the Ohio valley, passed through Indianapolis on its way to Illinois. At that time a road of stone and gravel was constructed along the first miles of today's Washington Street. Traffic picked up after construction of this road and a covered toll bridge across the White River.[2] A contemporary observer speaks of watching four-horse coaches and pioneer conestoga wagons laden with supplies and merchandise, and folks on foot and horseback "visible all day long at every point," all heading west along this road.[3] Soon a few small farms and homes appeared along the west bank of the river before beginning their slow spread inland. It was the beginning of a settlement that in early years was known as Indianola, but later became absorbed into the settled neighborhood of Stringtown.[4]

A few of Indianapolis' commercial elite purchased cheap tracts of land west of the river along the National Road hoping for a profit from an expected boom that did not materialize. One of those men, George Smith, publisher and editor of the city's first newspaper ("Indianapolis Gazette"), bought a farm about two miles west of the White River in a raised elevation of that area north of the National Road just east of the Little Eagle Creek. He named it Mount Jackson after his hero, President Andrew Jackson. His daughter Sarah, and her husband Nathaniel Bolton, inherited the farm and moved there in 1837.

In addition to managing the farm, by accounts an uphill struggle, they opened a tavern on their stretch of the National Road where a small settlement was beginning to form. They periodically hosted parties and dances for the local gentry, and for members of the Indiana General Assembly when they came in to hold session in the city. Not really typical of local farmers, both of them pursued their profession, he as a publisher and she as a poet (when she had time from managing the farm and tavern). Years later Sarah Bolton came to be known as the city's poet laureate.[5]

Also in 1837, W. C. Holmes built a public house and stables just south of the National Road in the same area, a response to growing numbers of visitors entering and leaving the city. A couple of stores followed shortly after in order to handle the needs of the few struggling farmers in the area as well as the needs of those passing through. The Boltons, meeting with local businessmen, decided to formally declare the existence of Mount Jackson village, named after the Bolton's farm. This little village of Mount Jackson, laid out and recorded in 1838, was located at the intersection of Warman and Washington Streets, the southwest corner of what is today considered the Hawthorne neighborhood.[6] Many years later one writer described the village as "the city's first suburb."[7]

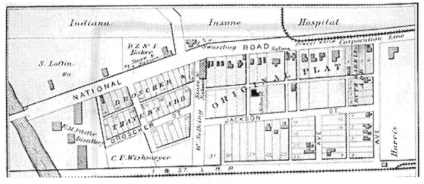

Figure 3 Mt. Jackson c. 1889

detail from Atlas of Indianapolis and Marion County, Gustav Bohn, Indiana, 1889. Indiana Historical Society

Mt. Jackson met the minimum expectations at that time for a small rural settlement—a couple of general stores, two taverns, one church (the Little Eagle Baptist Church), an elected town council, trustees and a sheriff, and a school that was the meeting place of most civic events in the area up until the end of the century.[8] The Boltons sold the Mt. Jackson farm in 1845 to the State of Indiana (for $5,300) where they constructed an asylum for the mentally handicapped. Over a year later the first of the buildings in the future medical complex of Central State Hospital was completed on the site of the old Bolton home. Central State, or the "Insane Institution" as it was referred to then, was an important institution in the city, frequently the brunt of local politics, and a beautiful towering landmark in the Mt. Jackson area. For many years it provided jobs for locals as well as attracting attention to the village itself and generating a small demand for local business. Mt. Jackson's permanence seemed assured by its location along the National Road and the growth of Indianapolis two miles to the east.

Shortly after the civil war the E. M. Pfeifer Distillery was opened close to Little Eagle Creek. A small cemetery was laid out by the earliest settlers about a quarter of a mile north of the village. The earliest headstones in Mt. Jackson Cemetery indicate burials dating to 1801, the period of early frontier settlement in the area. One of the founding families of the Mt. Jackson village is buried here, Sarah Harris, who died in 1842, and her husband Obedia who died in 1875.[9] The cemetery, on Tibbs Avenue just northwest of the grounds of the former Central State Hospital, is still maintained today.

Figure 4 Early Tomb Stones in Mt. Jackson Cemetery

In its early years Mount Jackson's leaders were known and active in Indianapolis society. Today there are few tangible reminders in the area of that early settlement: two streets named for founders and early residents (Harris and Warman), a Jackson Street, and the Mount Jackson Cemetery reflecting the town's name. Although you still find a few residents living in the Mt. Jackson area that would say they were from "Jacktown," a deeper knowledge of Mt. Jackson as a separate and viable community has disappeared.

CHAPTER 3

Economic Growth West of the River

The hoped for economic development of Indianapolis finally materialized after 1847 when the railroad coming up from Madison on the Ohio River finally reached the city, a first step towards the city becoming an important rail center. By 1855 there were eight railroads converging on the city that had transformed it into a transportation hub of national importance. Four of these railroads cut through the west side of the city: one north of Washington Street, the Indianapolis Bloomington & Western; and three to the south of Washington Street (the Indianapolis and St. Louis RR running just south of Mt. Jackson, the Terre Haute Vandalia and St. Louis RR further south, and the Indianapolis and Vincennes RR entering from the southwest (See fig. 2). These railroads had a strong economic and social impact upon the west side of the city and helped to fix emerging neighborhood boundaries by discouraging north-south movement.

During Mt. Jackson's early years, a rough two-mile trip along the National Road from the village into Indianapolis passed through open farmland before finally reaching a settlement that had begun to appear earlier on the west bank of the White River, the settlement that later became known as Stringtown.[10] Development began to take place along this strip in two areas south and north of the National Road: in West Indianapolis (Belmont), and in Haughville respectively. In 1862 Kingan, the Irish meat packing company, established stockyards and a meat-packing plant west of the White

River and south of Washington Street taking advantage of the undeveloped land and easy access to new railroads. A population of workers and businessmen quickly emerged around the stockyards. There were 471 residents when it first incorporated as the town of West Indianapolis in 1882, and 3,527 residents eight years later in the census.[11]

In the 1870s and 1880s industry moved into the westside of the city just north of the Indianapolis Bloomington & Western Railroad: National Malleable Castings arrived in 1875; Haugh & Co., a manufacturer of iron products, in1880; the Link-Belt Company in the 1880s. Other industries followed them, accompanied by smaller supportive enterprises. The area flourished.[12] A bustling community of homes and businesses emerged in the area north of Michigan Street, and in 1882 it incorporated as the town of Haughville.[13] The population of Haughville jumped from 70 in 1880 to 2,144 ten years later as workers poured in looking for jobs in the foundries and in new home construction. Railroad workers that had earlier settled in the area of Stringtown, mostly Irish and German, now began to be outnumbered by the flood of eastern Europeans (Slovenians) that settled in the Haughville area north of West Michigan Street. Michigan Street and the railroad emerged as a dividing line separating two very different ethnic groups and their neighborhoods.

When Haughville was incorporated in 1883, its official boundaries extended from Tenth Street south to the National Road (Washington Street) right up to Mt. Jackson, and from Belmont Avenue west to Tibbs.[14] But Haughville's actual development and its emerging population remained north of the Indianapolis Bloomington & Western Railroad (Michigan Street and north). There was no industrial development in Mt. Jackson, and the remaining area in between it and Haughville was still farmland.

The last two decades of the 19th century was a period of transformative change in Indianapolis. Peoples and businesses and industry poured into the city replacing the city's simpler frontier past with a new urban environment. Although growing traffic along the National Road had begun to link the residents of Mt. Jackson more closely with the life of Indianapolis, the village was too distant from the city's urban development to attract new populations. So Mt. Jackson did not grow much beyond its beginnings.

Nevertheless, evidence of Indianapolis' influence was apparent in Mt. Jackson. The Indianapolis Power and Light Company supplied the town with light and power. In 1882 the Citizens Street Railway Co. of Indianapolis extended its mule-car tracks along the National Road to the center of Mt. Jackson and then turned north to the Insane Institution where a turntable headed the car back towards the city (See fig.3). Local farmers and more distant visitors coming into the city from the west could now conveniently stable their horses more cheaply in Mt. Jackson and ride the trolleys into Indianapolis.[15]

In Mt. Jackson at this time there were about thirty families.[16] In 1889 the town's leaders met in Dorus Baker's grocery store and saloon and voted to incorporate (37 favored, 27 opposed). Wasting no time, the newly elected town board "adopted an ordinance for a $100 liquor license and a dog license, thus providing the necessary lubrication for the wheels of government."[17] Just nine years later, in 1897, all of the incorporated communities west of the White River, which included Mt. Jackson (and including Stringtown which had never incorporated), were annexed by the city of Indianapolis.[18]

At one of the last meetings before annexation, the Mt. Jackson board was still actively enforcing its own earlier initiatives, approving salary payments to board members and the Marshall, raising the taxes on residents to pay for water, the schoolhouse bond, and the cost of maintaining the road and the bridge across the Little Eagle Creek. Befitting a small village of this size, business was direct and personal, as board minutes reveal: "Jan. 15, 1897, moved and seconded that the sheriff notify John Walters to take out a liquor license or close up his place of business."[19] Things appeared to be picking up in the little village of Mt. Jackson. Yet one early 20th century observer about this time remarked that after all these years "there was not much of a town, and not much occasion for one."[20]

CHAPTER 4

From Farmland to Residential Settlement

By the 1870s a large corridor of unoccupied farmland belonging to the Enoch Warman family still stretched along the north side of the National Road (Washington Street), from Belmont Avenue west to Warman Avenue, and between Washington Street north to Vermont. (See fig.2.) In 1879 Enoch Warman sold this piece of land to his sister, Amanda Flack, wife of Joseph Flack, a successful Westside businessman. The promise of a growing population seeking land for residential construction west of the White River along the National Road presented an opportunity. The opening move in the rush to purchase a piece of Flack farmland was made by the Catholic Church.[21]

St. Anthony Church and School

In 1886 Bishop Silas Chatard of Vincennes, acting on a belief that there would be a need for a new parish to serve the expanding Haughville community, and anticipating the likelihood of new neighborhoods emerging in this general area, purchased a lot from Joseph and Amanda Flack in the northwest corner of the Flack farm (the corner of Vermont and Warman). A parish church-school was built and dedicated two years later in 1891 as St. Anthony

Parish School. In its first years it attracted about 400 members from the surrounding area, including Haughville and Stringtown. An additional plot was purchased from the Flacks in 1897 for the construction of a convent and a church (completed in 1904).[22]

Figure 5 St. Anthony Church and Church School c.1904

Indiana Historical Society, P0411

St. Anthony's purchase was followed almost immediately by a group of land speculators from the Indianapolis Land and Improvement Company who wanted to make a quick profit on the sale of lots near the church. The whole area had been annexed to Indianapolis in 1897 and they anticipated an increase in land values. They paid $5,800 for sixty-five acres from the Flack estate in 1900 for residential development. They laid out 380 lots on this acreage from Vermont Street down to Washington Street, and Warman Avenue West to Belleview, naming it "West Park Addition." The small town of Mt. Jackson was located at the extreme southwest corner of this new addition, separated from the new addition by a busy Washington Street. A few years later, in 1908, Trotter & Henry Company purchased the rest of the Flack property and surveyed

239 more plots from Mount Street to Belmont Avenue, joining the Trotter & Henry Addition to the older West Park Addition. The majority of the lots in both additions were 40' X 140' and sold for $200 each. Larger lots measuring 40' X 175' were laid out along the north side of Washington Street and sold for $300 each. The new West Park Addition began to fill quickly with homes that were "more substantial than those built north of Vermont Street" in Haughville, a fact that later contributed to a "better than" feeling among some Hawthorne residents.[23]

In the years before World War I, the availability of over six hundred residential lots produced a flurry of home and church construction in this new residential area. Initially this new development was expected to encourage a rush of residential overflow from Haughville. From the start, however, the West Park and the Trotter & Henry additions attracted a different population and developed independently (and quite differently) from both Haughville and Stringtown.

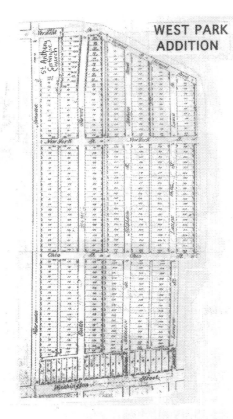

Figure 6 West Park Sub-Division Plot Map 1901-02

Indiana Marion County Recorders Office, Indianapolis, IN

A flood of new institutions appeared in order to serve this population—churches, a school, a library, and a few businesses. Many of these prewar structures remain today as part of the physical profile of the early emerging Hawthorne community.[24] They were: St. Anthony Catholic Church and School, Hawthorne School (#50), West Park Christian Church, Washington Street United Methodist Church, and the Hawthorne Library, all built before World War I.

Hawthorne School (School #50)

When Indianapolis annexed Mt. Jackson in 1897, their little red brick schoolhouse became School #50 of the Indianapolis Public Schools system (IPS). At that time the old school building (on Jackson Street) was apparently a fairly unpleasant place "with doors which rattled with the slightest breeze, windows minus panes, whose vacancies were stuffed with papers and old rags."[25] Clearly it had been neglected, and in any case was inadequate for the growing residential population appearing north of Washington Street. In 1904, the same year that St. Anthony's was completed, a new School #50 was constructed on North Germania Avenue (name changed to Belleview in 1917) further east and just north of Washington Street in the heart of the new West Park Addition. The new school, named "Nathaniel Hawthorne School" (School #50) after the famous American writer, consisted of: five classrooms that served grades 1-6, a principal's office, a teachers' room, and a combination gym and stage that occupied the second floor. This was a vast improvement over the old Mount Jackson School, although in the first few years pupils of the 7th and 8th grades had to attend School #16 further east on West Market Street in Stringtown. When the seventh and eighth grades were finally added to School #50 in 1912, the school graduated its first 8th grade class. The school's growth in the years following its founding reflected the rapid residential growth taking place in this area and a shift away from Mount Jackson as the area's focal point.[26]

Figure 7 Hawthorne School (IPS School #50) c. 1904

Indiana Historical Society, Bass Photo Co. Collection

West Park Christian Church

In 1904, a very busy year in the new subdivision, the Indianapolis Disciples of Christ worshipers held a large four-week tent revival meeting on North Addison Street just one block west of the Hawthorne School in what was coming to be known as the West Park Addition. During that gathering a core of followers organized a Bible School with help from its sister churches in Indianapolis. Out of their efforts a permanent church congregation was established, the West Park Christian Church, with fifty founding members, an Elder, three Deacons, and a Clerk. But it was a congregation without a church building. This newly formed congregation held its first service in the old Mount Jackson schoolhouse in October of that year and began to search for a place to build a church. Once the congregation had recruited a permanent pastor and the decision to build was made enthusiasm and commitment took over. In 1906 the completed church was dedicated at 24 N. Addison where it now stands. Their numbers grew rapidly.[27]

Figure 8 West Park Christian Church in the 1990s

Washington Street United Methodist Church

The founding of the West Washington Street Methodist Episcopal Church nearby (later to become the Washington Street United Methodist Church) was also a response to the new sub-division and to the families that were moving into the area. However, the initiative for building this church came from residents of the much older Mt. Jackson community. In 1888 the Tabernacle Presbyterian Church from Indianapolis had organized a Mission Sunday School in Mount Jackson village in the old brick schoolhouse. The village had about thirty families at this time, but no Church or Sunday school. They quickly outgrew the schoolhouse, so the Tabernacle Church helped them build a little white frame church with a belfry in 1889 in the 2900 block of West Washington Street.

As new families joined their meetings, Methodists began to outnumber the Presbyterians. The nearest Methodist church was further north across the tracks on King Avenue and inconvenient to attend. So the congregation voted in 1897 to become Methodist. They purchased land in 1904 at the corner of West Washington and Warman, and the little white frame church with belfry was moved to its new (current) location. For the next fifteen years the congregation grew primarily from the families settling in the new West Park Addition. Numbers became so great that chairs had to be placed in the aisles to accommodate expanding numbers, so they decided to rebuild. In 1919 they tore down the frame church and began a new building on the same property. They laid a cornerstone in 1920, and in 1924 dedicated the current imposing brick structure on that corner (See fig. 28).[28]

Hathorne Library

In 1911 the Carnegie Foundation funded the building of a library on donated property at Mount and Ohio Streets only a few yards from the Hawthorne School that had been completed just seven years earlier. Taking its name from the school, it became the Hawthorne Branch Library of the Indianapolis Public Library system. (See figs. 9 and 19.) The city's choice of location was rather surprising since the area to be served was not very large or populous. Its construction was a testament to an emerging sense of community among new residents and the determination of leaders from the several churches and schools who made a case for future community growth and support.[29] These were times of rapid development on the Westside, so the case was likely not difficult to make.

Hawthorne Library quickly became much more than a library. It played an important role in defining this new pre-war community by functioning for several years as a community center and a meeting place where all kinds of activities took place, including various kinds of socials, business meetings, Hawthorne School PTA meetings, school plays, and even basketball games! It was considered "a model community library."[30]

Figure 9 1925 Graduating Class of Hawthorne School

(in front of Hawthorne Library)

CHAPTER 5

Immigrants and Cultural Differences Before World War I

Industrial activity was in full swing in Indianapolis towards the end of the century as ten thousand passengers a day came and went through the newly completed (1888) Union Railway Station. Immigrants poured into the city for jobs doubling its population between 1880 and 1900 reflecting a national as well as a local pattern of dramatic growth and development.[31] Many of these new arrivals sought cheap housing on the Westside near the railroad shops and factories where they now worked—boarding houses or rental rooms for single males, and small cottages for families if they could afford them. The Germans and Irish settled in the Stringtown area. Macedonians, Hungarians, Poles, and Slovenians settled mostly north of Michigan Street in Haughville.[32] As the dominant group in Haughville, the Slovenians shaped that bustling community through development of schools and businesses as well as cultural institutions, until the onset of changes during World War II.

The quiet lifestyle of the older Mt. Jackson, as well as the new West Park sub-division emerging nearby in the remaining farmland, was a stark contrast to Haughville that had smaller houses on smaller lots, and a much larger and more ethnically diverse population. The men from the Mt. Jackson and West Park area worked together side by side in the foundry and on the railroads with those from Haughville, but they went home to different neighborhoods. Differences between these communities sometimes became conflicts, not an uncommon occurrence in Indianapolis at this time. Life in St. Anthony's Church offers an illustration of how these differences could escalate.[33]

In the 1890s and early 1900s, St. Anthony's was the closest Catholic Church for many families in the area, and it was predominantly Irish. The Catholic immigrant groups from Haughville further north were drawn to worship at St. Anthony's making its congregation more culturally diverse. Although this diversity was normally managed by having each ethnic group organize their own clubs and organizations, the differences sometimes generated conflict. Slovenians from Haughville attending St. Anthony's didn't know English, preventing them from participating in the full life of what they called "the Irish church." They were committed Catholics, however, and organized two religious lodges of their own through which they continued to support the parish enthusiastically.

But there were other cultural differences besides language. Though the Catholic Church was not officially against drinking, the temperance movement had taken strong hold in the West Park area, and at St. Anthony's. The outspoken pastor's attempt to discourage excessive drinking and occasions for it clashed with the Slovenian lifestyle that could not imagine social occasions without it. These differences of social behavior and language reached a breaking point in 1905. The Slovenians held a dance to help pay off the church's debt, but they did so without the pastor's permission. When it was learned that an Irish girl from West Park had gotten drunk at the party the pastor's reaction was so severe that many of the Slovenians refused to attend mass at St. Anthony's and began to push for a separate national parish.

Ultimately their demands were successful. In 1907 Holy Trinity Church was dedicated in Haughville, and the majority of Slovenes left St. Anthony's for Holy Trinity. The boundary between the two parishes was established at Vermont Street, paralleling the railroad tracks, thus reinforcing a distinction that was already emerging between the older Haughville and the new West Park Addition.[34] Some in Haughville were not attracted to Holy Trinity and continued to attend St. Anthony's that now drew its membership predominantly from the new West Park area. Rapid development in the neighborhood allowed St. Anthony's to recover its membership quickly.

In 1913, normal life on the Westside was shattered when a levy on the White River broke and swept through the city during the worst flood in the state's history. The neighborhoods of Stringtown and West Indianapolis were hit hard. The river crested at 19.5 feet above flood stage leaving some areas of Indianapolis under thirty-one feet of water. Houses, "car barns" (for the Indianapolis Transit System), and Stringtown's School #16 were all under water. Floodwaters reached as far west as Belmont Avenue covering the area called "The Valley" all the way up to "The Hill," the high ground east of Belmont near the Belt Railroad.

But the floodwaters did not directly impact the newer residential area west of Belmont Avenue, the street that marked the eastern boundary of the newly developing West Park area. Roughly three million [1913] dollars of damage was done, but remarkably only eight people died. Nonetheless, housing was devastated. Some have argued that Stringtown never quite recovered from that flood, another factor that distinguished it from the newer West Park neighborhood to its west.[35]

CHAPTER 6

World War I, 1914-1918

Since the U. S. was late to enter the war (early 1917), its impact upon the heartland in terms of loss of life was not so great. A number of young men from the Westside went off to war, but few lost their lives. Of the one hundred and fifteen young men that served in the war from St. Anthony's, for instance, six died in the war.[36] Nonetheless, war fever swept the state and reached into the Westside neighborhoods in a number of other ways, including rationing, and the sale of Liberty Bonds, and reactions against German immigrants. A large military encampment was set up in an open field that had been used as an occasional fairground, a few years later to become the site of George Washington High School.

Despite the fact that non-native ethnic groups have always been a vital part of Indianapolis history, including the Westside, nativist feelings emerged with force during World War I. "Americanization" campaigns had an impact on every facet of life from politics and religion to public education. Loyalty oaths were required of teachers, and German language was banned from school curricula. There were a number of families of German descent in the Westside, some having arrived in the U. S. many years before, and some more recently. Non-naturalized German residents were actually identified in the *Indianapolis Star* opening them up to attack.[37] The names of two streets that ran through the Westside neighborhoods were changed to avoid any reference to Germany: Bismarck Avenue became Pershing Avenue, and Germania Avenue became

24

Belleview Place.[38] It takes little effort to imagine the social challenge confronting some families during this period, particularly since many of them had been very vocal in their support of Germany before the U. S. entered the war.

The war encouraged suspicion of difference and radical behavior in all its forms. In the post-war years that suspicion contributed to the "100% Americanism" campaign throughout the country and to the anti-Catholic and anti-Jewish appeal of the Ku Klux Klan in the 1920s. Nevertheless the post-war years were prosperous for the whole city. Businesses, industry and rail traffic all expanded. And there was no interruption of the bustling pre-war growth in the West Park area.

CHAPTER 7

An Emerging Identity Between the Wars

Even before World War I the hub of activity in the neighborhood had begun to shift from Mt. Jackson to the new West Park suburb that was starting to develop its own rhythms. Small neighborhood businesses had opened between Belmont and Tibbs to meet the needs of the new residents: grocery stores, pharmacies, two doctors' offices, a few bars. Most of the residents were recent arrivals and shared the enthusiasm that often accompanies new beginnings.

Home construction began in earnest in the first decade of the century and continued on into the 1920s and 1930s. Slowly a new neighborhood began to appear shaped by the opportunities and activities offered by churches, schools, businesses, the library, and various social groups. The neighborhood's boundaries had become clear to residents, and this new suburb was emerging as a distinct community, although it was not yet clear just what the character or the name of that community would be. Those questions were answered between the two world wars. The beginning of a local newspaper played a major role in shaping that change.

"West Side Messenger"

In 1915, while the war was in its early stages in Europe and prior to U. S. entry, a Disciples of Christ pastor, Clarence Garfield Baker, arrived with his family to assume the pastorate of the thriving new West Park Christian Church. A graduate of Hiram College in Ohio and the University of Chicago where he had earned his M.A. degree, Rev. Baker was what was commonly called a "good catch" for this growing congregation. Everywhere he turned in the new neighborhood from which most of his parishioners were drawn he encountered enthusiasm, and he was excited by the opportunities presented at his new post. Before a year passed, in addition to his pastoral responsibilities, Baker had founded the Westside's first newspaper, the *West Side Christian Messenger* (soon to be renamed "West Side Messenger"). Its purpose was "to honestly and faithfully boost for those things that help build a progressive neighborhood and to tie together the schools, churches, business and social agencies for the good of all."[39]

Charles Guthrie and Diane Arnold

West Side Messenger

Vol. XII   Indianapolis, Indiana, November 11, 1927   No. 32

West Park Church To Hold Community Banquet

On Tuesday evening, November 15, from 6:00 to 9:00, the West Park Men's Bible Class will sponsor a community banquet to which they are inviting the business and professional men and women of the community.

The general theme of the evening will be "A Better Community in Which to Work and Live." Rev. N. L. Collins, of Princeton, who has been called to be the new pastor of that church, will be toastmaster. The music will be in charge of Frank Buster. Among well-known men who are on the program are Elmer W. Stout, Fletcher American National Bank; Prof. W. G. Gingery, of Washington High School; Mr. George P. Terrence, manager of the Link-Belt Company, and Harry Kelley, attorney.

The dinner will be a fried chicken dinner. Price, 50 cents.

Hawthorne House Activities

Girls' Basketball

...

WASHINGTON HIGH SCHOOL
To Be Dedicated Wednesday, November 16th.

W. G. GINGERY, Principal

MRS. GAUL, Dean of Girls

WASHINGTON HIGH SCHOOL DEDICATION

The new Washington High School will be formally dedicated next Wednesday, November 16th.

WASHINGTON HIGH WILL PLAY THE LAST GAME OF THE SEASON

WASHINGTON HIGH SCHOOL

D. A. R. PRESENTED FLAG TO WASHINGTON HIGH

West Washington Street Presbyterian Church

T. J. Simpson, Pastor

Memorial Baptist Church

West Michigan Street Methodist Episcopal Church

Danner Brothers Are Enlarging Their Store

West Park Chrisian Church

Addison and West Washington St.

West Washington Street Methodist Episcopal Church

L. B. Kendall, Pastor

St. Paul's Reformed Church

John H. Buoch, Pastor

Well Known Local Citizen Dies

West Side Boy Scout Notes

Calvary Presbyterian Church

Six West Side Teams In Basketball

Figure 10 Front Page of 1927 West Side Messenger

In the beginning Baker composed the weekly four-page paper in his own home at 201 N. Addison in the heart of the (later named)

Hawthorne community. He had 3,000 copies of the paper printed up on Michigan Street and distributed free to residents in the area. The paper was funded by advertisements from Westside businesses. The *Messenger* brought to people's attention the daily happenings in their own community, something the Indianapolis papers did not do. In Baker's own words: "It enables the desirable elements in a community, such as the churches, schools, social clubs, businesses and industries to get their messages to the people. A paper fosters community spirit and cohesiveness."[40] The primary target of the paper in its early years under Baker's management, particularly the social news, remained predominantly in his own neighborhood. As the paper's circulation increased, however, it targeted surrounding neighborhoods as well.

A section of the paper entitled "Local" announced community activities that did not warrant a full article: "The Hawthorne School of Expression is planning for its annual Christmas play . . . " Or personals: "The Schilling family have moved from 242 North Addison to 201 North Tremont;" and "Mr. Raymond Lee Jones will sing over Radio Station UFBM . . ."[41] As its founder had intended, the paper gave voice to local organizations and individuals, and helped to mobilize support for issues of importance to the community.

Though politics was not the most important focus of Baker's paper, when issues arose or it came time for elections he was not shy about using an editor's prerogative to share his political position, one that was clearly progressive and Democratic. For instance, in the 1920s when the Ku Klux Klan dominated the city as well as the Hawthorne community, his editorials attacked the widespread intolerance, a stance that likely cost him his position as pastor of the large West Park Christian Church.[42]

In the 1930s, Baker strongly supported Roosevelt's New Deal that challenged the political system in Indianapolis and the state that was, he argued, dominated by an elite minority hostile to working class interests. In a lengthy and scathing front page editorial in 1934 entitled "The New Deal Challenge to Marion County Democracy," Baker slams the Marion County Republicans and calls on the Democratic Party to support the New Deal and organize against a Republican establishment.[43] By the mid-thirties the paper claimed a circulation of over 8,000. Its expanded audience was reflected in the articles and advertisements.[44]

Hawthorne Community Center/ Hawthorne House

In the middle of the newly emerging West Park community in the early 1920s was an organization deeply committed to serving residents, the West Park Social Service Association, renamed Hawthorne Social Service Association soon after its founding. In retrospect this was the first of the community's two defining moments.[45] The second was the founding of George Washington High School. The leadership of these two initiatives was closely linked.

The history of the founding and early years of the Hawthorne Social Service Association reflects much about the community it was to serve.[46] In the prosperous years after the war, rumors began to circulate that some undeveloped lots just north of the Hawthorne Library and Hawthorne School #50, between Ohio Street and Turner Avenue, were going to be purchased by the nearby railroad and used as a switchyard, or possibly a coal dump. This strip known locally as "Flack's Pasture," a reference to Joseph Flack, the owner of the farmland upon which the community was built, was located in the heart of the neighborhood. Even though it was private land, it was a clean open space, a welcome playground for children, and at that time referred to as "Miniature Park." The neighborhood was already bounded on north and south by rail lines, a fact that residents had become accustomed to and even embraced as clear boundaries that identified the limits of their community. But if the railroad was allowed to go ahead with its project, it would be a noisy and dirty intrusion into the heart of their community.

Feelings against the railroad project were running high in 1921 when about fifty women and men gathered in the basement of the Hawthorne Library to discuss how to deal with this threat. They established the West Park Community Association (soon to be renamed Hawthorne Community Association) and began pursuing the possibility of purchasing that land on behalf of the community.

An early photo of the Association's Board of Directors reflects a wide range of local talent and a leadership that remained deeply involved in the work of the neighborhood for many years. From left to right, back row: Robert Groth, Mrs. Charles Perrine, Mrs. R. H. Fletemeyer, W. E. Vantalge, Mrs. E. C. Carsten, Walter G. Gingery, Mrs. Oscar Jones, Mrs. Charles Gooden, Mrs. James Boyd, Curtis Crist; left to right front row seated: Dr. E. R. Gaddy, Mrs. J. W. Carter, Mrs. Alma R. Lemen, Dr. L. M. Sartor, Rev. C. G. Baker, Miss Hazel Smith, and Miss Mary Harmon.

Figure 11 Hawthorne Community Association Board

In the meetings that followed the Association also discussed the need for a community center from which to coordinate and house neighborhood events and activities, a place for various organizations to hold their meetings, and a place where especially the children of the neighborhood could focus their energies and at the same time be supervised and guided.

Association members were familiar with the work of Christamore House, a social experiment operating since 1905 on the north side of the city near Butler University, that attempted to address the needs of foreign born and working class residents such as healthcare, child care for working mothers, English, and other programs to prepare them for citizenship. (Christamore House soon moved to Haughville.) Yet Hawthorn's situation was quite different.

Hawthorne was a homogeneous American blue-collar working class population. There were very few immigrants or impoverished residents in their neighborhood. Nonetheless, Hawthorne leaders were impressed by the concept of a community center around which a variety of community activities could be organized and moral precepts taught. The Hawthorne Library, a frequent meeting place in the early years, was inadequate for such demands. Nor was there a high school in the area that might serve that purpose. So they decided to build a community center on the property they were pursuing, and they formed the West Park Social Service Association to oversee it. This association was officially certified by the Secretary of State on July 26, 1923, with prominent local businessman Charles H. Royster as President and Rev. Clarence G. Baker as Executive Director, both of whom served in their positions for the next quarter century.

Executive Director Baker was instructed to immediately begin raising funds for purchase of the land thereby preventing the railroad from doing so, and then "to erect, equip, and maintain a community house, plan and supervise activities there, cooperate with the Board of Directors, and prepare a monthly report in writing." The goals of the Association, soon after renamed the Hawthorne Social Services Association, were lofty. As stated in the association's constitution, the purpose was "to operate a community center to provide recreational opportunities and to develop skills and attitudes which will improve the citizenship, ideals, and individual moral, ethical, educational, and social responsibilities of its members in the community."[47]

Ultimately funding for the land and the building was raised largely by small subscriptions from individual residents, and from local community and business organizations, a remarkable demonstration of community spirit and vision. Baker was so

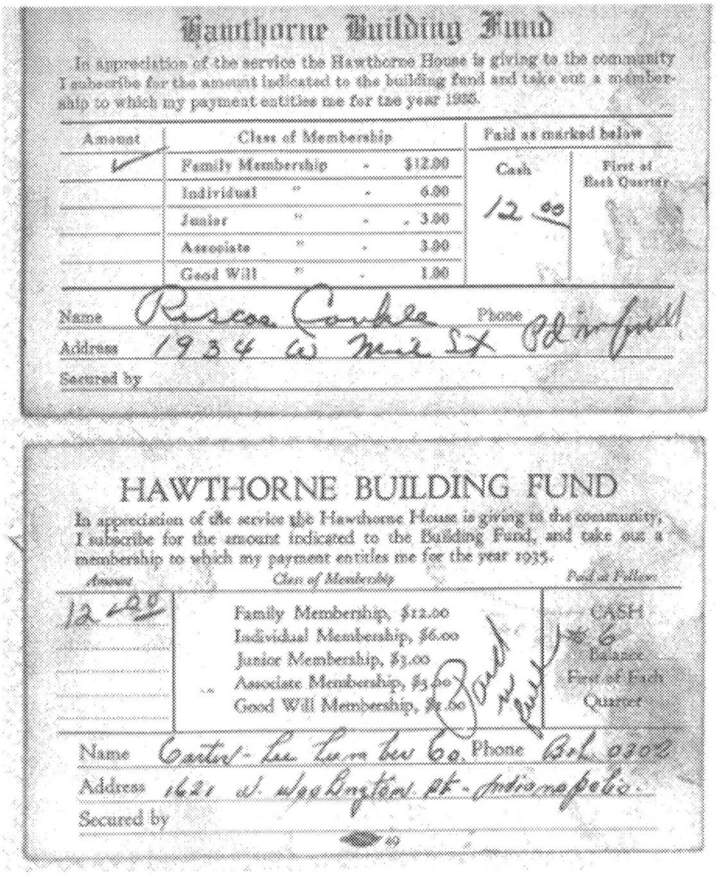

Hawthorne Building Fund

In appreciation of the service the Hawthorne House is giving to the community I subscribe for the amount indicated to the building fund and take out a membership to which my payment entitles me for the year [illegible].

Amount	Class of Membership		Paid as marked below	
			Cash	First of Each Quarter
✓	Family Membership	$12.00	12 00	
	Individual "	6.00		
	Junior "	3.00		
	Associate "	3.00		
	Good Will "	1.00		

Name Roscoe Conkle Phone [illegible]

Address 1934 W Mich St

Secured by

HAWTHORNE BUILDING FUND

In appreciation of the service the Hawthorne House is giving to the community, I subscribe for the amount indicated to the Building Fund, and take out a membership to which my payment entitles me for the year [illegible].

Amount	Class of Membership	Paid as Follows
12 00	Family Membership, $12.00 Individual Membership, $6.00 Junior Membership, $3.00 Associate Membership, $3.00 Good Will Membership, $1.00	CASH Balance First of Each Quarter

Name Carter-Lee Lumber Co. Phone [illegible]

Address 1621 W. Washington St.-Indianapolis

Secured by

Figure 12 Hawthorne House Membership Cards

successful in securing funds that seven months later, on March 2, 1924, the stucco and frame eight room building known as Hawthorne House (later known as the Hawthorne Community Center), located at 2440 Ohio Street on the southern tip of "Flack's pasture," was dedicated in its own gym-auditorium packed with community members as well as representatives from Indianapolis.[48]

The Hawthorne Center was an immediate and popular success, but not without its challenges. At this time the Ku Klux Klan had become quite active in the neighborhood, as it was throughout the city. During the dedication ceremony a spokesman for the Klan approached Rev. Baker and offered a substantial contribution to the building fund if the Klan would be allowed to hold its meeting there.

When Baker refused the request, about half of the audience (total estimated attendance was 600) stood up by pre-arranged signal and walked out of the meeting in protest. Given Rev. Baker's anti-Klan editorials in the *Messenger,* and his public stand against the Klan just days earlier at West Park Christian Church, there was concern that this latest rebuff might affect the level of support for the Center.[49] For half of them to walk out in protest against Baker's latest response shows the very deep divisions that had been generated by the Klan activity in the neighborhood. But the community's positive response in the form of memberships and donations in the days that followed quickly put an end to their concerns. Years later, in response to a reporter's question about his rejection of the Klan offer, Baker responded simply, "We thought Hawthorne should be dedicated to racial and religious liberty."[50]

Local support for the Center was obvious. Memberships jumped from 450 in January of 1924 (before the dedication), to over 1,800 by 1935. In that same eleven-year period, attendance at the Center's activities increased from 1,525 in December of 1923 to 6,135 in December of 1935.[51] Each dollar bought a share in the Center. Hawthorne Center really belonged to the community. Many of those who moved out of the neighborhood in later years retained their membership. They considered it *their* Center and accordingly maintained that connection.

Shortly after the founding of the Center the Hawthorne Social Service Association also purchased two additional properties: one just west of the Center was a house they referred to as the Annex; a second house to the east was called the Cottage. The Annex for years was

**Figure 13 Sketch of the Hawthorne Social
Service Association Buildings**

used for children's activities, including a free kindergarten. The Cottage served as a place for adult activities such as meetings, offices for permanent staff, and later in the sixties and seventies as the central office for the Indianapolis Settlements, Inc. (ISI).[52]

Immediately across the street to the south of these three buildings belonging to the Hawthorne Association was Hawthorne School (IPS School #50), and Hawthorne Library. Five buildings, all associated with the name "Hawthorne," housed a staggering array of activities and services offered to the Hawthorne neighborhood, and sometimes beyond. A 1949 article in the "Messenger" commemorating 25 years of service by the Association began with: "Scarcely a West Sider exists, that does not have fond youthful memories of games and activities held in the quarter-century old Hawthorne Community House, on West Ohio Street."[53]

The Hawthorne Center's service area at that time was bounded on the north by the B & O Railroad yards, on the south by the Pennsylvania Railroad yards, on the east by the Belt Railroad, and on the west by Eagle Creek and the city limits ---- an area with an estimated population in 1934 of 10,000. It was described as "a working people's neighborhood, but not a slum district." The focus of the Hawthorne Association's work was comprehensive and soon provided "a full program of welfare, recreational and moral educational activities" from kindergarten through high school, with a large number of clubs for boys and girls of all ages such as the Brownie Club, the Cub Club, Wolfe Club, Girl Scouts, Boy Scouts, Girl Reserves, and many others.

By 1930, 61 different organizations held meetings at the Center. The Center hosted a thriving kindergarten in its Annex. The Center even fielded a small orchestra at this time.[54] In 1934 the Association had 1500 members. It cooperated with other local organizations and with the city of Indianapolis to improve the community. The Center served a neighborhood that by the mid-1930s had already become defined in most residents' minds as "Hawthorne." It took pride in its motto: "Hawthorne: The Good Neighbor of Its Community in the Heart of the Great West Side."[55]

Figure 14 The First Hawthorne House, c. 1930

One of the most popular places, especially in the winter, was the Center's gymnasium. Hawthorne Center fielded about twenty basketball teams from the neighborhood that competed regularly at the gymnasium, reflecting the "Hoosier hysteria" of the times, and "many a hot game was staged on the floor while larger and enthusiastic galleries made the rafters ring with their cheers."[56] Director Baker's vision for the whole community was embodied in the Center. Not only was it a place for exercise and education, he explained, "but it is a social center as well, where old and young can gather and get acquainted with their neighbors. It is a bond that pulls people closer together, for it is their own, not merely a public building. Our ultimate goal is to have every person in the neighborhood an active member of our association."[57]

The Hawthorne Center became an important hub of daily life. With this institution and its leadership in place, participation in its programs and activities helped to create a neighborhood with a strong social fabric and civic pride---a community. It continued its role through the good years of the fifties and sixties, through the years of creeping neighborhood decline in the seventies and eighties, and into the more recent times of challenge and renewal. Even though the focus of programs and services sometimes changed, the original purpose of the center did not change over the years---the building and nurturing of community in the neighborhood.[58]

George Washington High School

What finally cast a mantel of common vision and social networks over the Hawthorne neighborhood, and strengthening links with nearby neighborhoods, was the founding of George Washington High School (GWHS). While the building of the Community Center was underway, the Hawthorne Association was also talking about the need for more neighborhood schooling and had been lobbying the Indianapolis Public School System to build a high school on the Westside. Their arguments were strong.

The recorded population of the Westside in 1922 was 42,000. At this time approximately 670 students qualified for high school, but only about 60 actually graduated each year owing mainly to the practical hurdle of distance from the closest school. Since this rapidly growing area had no high school, students wishing to pursue their studies had to take the streetcar to the center of the city, and then take a transfer to one of the three high schools in the city: Shortridge, Arsenal Tech, or Manual. This effectively discouraged all but the most dedicated. Popular demand from the Westside was joined by support from public opinion and organizations in the city.

Finally, in April of 1922, representatives from the Hawthorne Association, the Hawthorne PTA, and the editor of the *West Side Messenger* went before the city's School Commissioners with their proposal. The plan was approved. The School Board purchased 12 ½ acres of land in Hawthorne on the south side of Washington Street between Tremont and Sheffield Avenues, an open field that had for years been used as a fairground (and a military encampment during World War I), and drew up plans for the school. Construction began in 1925 and finished in September of 1926, just in time for the first class to attend. The school opened with 38 teachers and 874 students. Head of the Math Department at Shortridge High School, Walter Gingery, became the first Principal and served for the next twenty-five years until his retirement in 1951.[59]

In the early years enrollment increased more than 100 students a year forcing the construction of temporary buildings until a permanent addition was completed in 1937. The school's educational and social offerings continued to meet the needs of a growing Westside, and for many years George Washington High School supplied the city, and beyond, with leadership in all of the professions, and with competitive sports teams.

Figure 15 Aerial View of George Washington High School c. 1930.jpg

Washington High School was different from other schools in the city. It was begun as a community project, led in large part by the same community leaders that had founded the Hawthorne Center. (The Rev. C. G. Baker was sometimes referred to as "the father of George Washington High School."). It was a community school that served the Westside. "And as a 'child' of the community," wrote the *Indianapolis News* in 1929, "the school has, and merits, the unwavering support and co-operation of residents of the west side."[60] Whereas other high schools drew students from all parts of the city, the students attending Washington, particularly in the early years, came from the immediate area: the neighborhoods of Hawthorne, Haughville, and Stringtown. Since the school was actually located on the eastern edge of the newly forming West Park/Hawthorne community, the school grew hand-in-glove with that community.

Equally important was the school's focus on goals and activities that the different neighborhoods could share, whether the arts or academics or athletics. Rev. Baker highlighted these contributions in a talk given to the George Washington Men's Club in 1934. A reporter from the *West Side Messenger* summarized his talk.

> Mr. Baker said in part that the school was first of all a unifying influence in creating community loyalty and unity throughout the entire west side . . . He said that as an educational factor in the development of the west side the school had brought about a decided change in the entire community . . . Eight years ago it was so unusual for any of our west side young people to graduate from college that it was made an item of special interest, but since the establishment of the High School, almost 200 young people have gone to college and practically all of the better colleges [in] Indiana have from 2 to 15 Washington graduates enrolled in their student body. Some of these students have graduated with high honors and have already taken their place in the civic and industrial life of the Westside. The educational standard of this part of the city has been greatly raised.[61]

In addition to the pressures of a rigorous academic program, there were football games, basketball games, plays, music performances, contests, various competitions with other city schools, clubs of various types, and easy access to the school's teachers and administrators. Shared school activities created a kind of common social agenda throughout the Westside. Differences between the neighborhoods continued, but they tended to take a back seat to school activities. The same was true between students. One Hawthorne student who attended Washington High School in the 1920s recalled that as young people were forced to talk to one another they discovered that the gang members they had feared from other neighborhoods had also feared them. They found that amusing.[62]

Walking to and from school was easy, and confronting the flow of school traffic became part of the area's daily social ritual. As the school routine and extra-curricular offerings began to order lives and dominate conversations, local families assumed a kind of ownership of this new institution. Parents who heretofore had not given much thought to secondary education now were unable to avoid the visible presence of this large building that housed constant activity and added new layers of interaction and shared experience. The school also brought awareness of the Westside to the attention of the city and beyond through the achievements of its students and the quality of its programs and faculty.

The GWHS faculty and coaching staff were committed professionals, a number of whom had reputations in the state and beyond. They remained at the school for many years providing program continuity and personal links with families in the community.[63] A few lived near the school and knew parents and students in non-school settings, thus cementing their commitment to the community's welfare. Thelma Flack, one of the early students from the area to graduate from Washington, in the class of 1929, offers a good illustration of this commitment. After receiving her teaching certificate at Butler University she married and returned to teach in the school. She attributed her success to the teachers who had given her such personal attention and encouragement, and she modeled her own career after them.[64] She lived in the Westside area and worked at Washington High School into the 1970s.

Life in the 1920s and 1930s

Most of the 1920s was a prosperous period for Indianapolis, with ample work and opportunity for residents and newcomers alike. The population of Indianapolis had tripled between 1890 and 1920, from 105,000 to 314,000,[65] and the city developed other suburbs such as Speedway City, Mars Hill, and University Heights in the south. West Indianapolis absorbed the town of Belmont and became known by that name.[66] Neighborhoods throughout the city remained mostly stable.

Daily Life

In the West Park/Hawthorne neighborhood church membership rolls were expanding, as were the number of new homes. The streets were gradually paved. House construction seemed constant, though the neighborhood still had a few open spaces marked by "cut throughs" that served as playgrounds for kids until new homebuilders occupied them. This was a White working class neighborhood, with two-parent close-knit families each with two or three kids, sometimes joined by grandparents. Fathers went to work every day, generally in the factories just beyond the neighborhood. Most moms stayed home becoming volunteers at the church and the Community Center, Cub Scout leaders, and managers of the "home front," a term made popular during the Great War.

Weekdays were ordered by rotating work shifts at the nearby factories (J. D. Adams, Duesenberg, Link-Belt Company, National Malleable, Haugh, Ketcham & Co., Kingan & Co.) and by the whistle blasts of long trains passing west-east through the Westside and converging on the city at frequent and predictable intervals. That, together with a wide range of community activities, lent an air of stability and promise. The Indianapolis Bloomington & Western R. R. coming from the northwest and the Indianapolis & St. Louis R. R. coming from directly west helped to define neighborhood and social boundaries.

There were new inventions, new styles in dress, new dances, and the accompanying new social behaviors to challenge traditions. Cars were the newest technological distraction, and ownership of a Marmon or a Cole or an Overland was generally a clear indication of economic status in the community. The Duesenberg plant was located just west of Mt. Jackson along Washington Street at Harding Street, and the straight stretch along Washington Street the length of the Hawthorne neighborhood was used to road test the cars. All enjoyed the minor dramas created by this show of the promising new technology. Electric trolley tracks ran west down the middle of Washington Street before turning around at the loop at Tibbs and heading back east. On the weekends families boarded the trolley cars for downtown shopping, or transferred to a line that would take them to Riverside Park or Broad Ripple or other popular destinations in the city. [67]

The *West Side Messenger,* published weekly in the heart of Hawthorne, kept everybody informed of the latest happenings in the area. Since a number of parishioners and students lived in Haughville and Speedway, the paper now included some news and advertisements from those areas as well, mostly from Haughville's busy Michigan Street on the northern edge of Hawthorne. The *Messenger*'s advertisements from local businesses reinforced the sense of community. These owners were folks that lived and worked in the community: Dorsey's Grocery, Peck's Grocery, T. J. Simpson Chiropractor, Manring Pharmacy, Belmont Pharmacy, Van Talge Hardware, Belmont State Bank, Brown's Dry Goods Store, Royster & Askin Funeral Directors, George W. Usher Funeral Director, Belmont Furniture Store, Robey Motor Car Company, Addison Cleaners, and more.[68]

**Figure 16 Advertisments from the West Side
Messenger, November 16, 1934**

In the late evening when the weather was pleasant folk would
promenade through the neighborhood after work and dinner.

Houses were built near the street and residents could often visit with passersby from the comfort of their front porch or front steps. Looking back from a 1962 perspective, an older resident remembered community life in those earlier years. The owner of Stout's Drugstore at the corner of south Addison and Washington "was a friend of the whole community. His store was a meeting place. The men used to go there in the evenings to buy cigars." Next door to Stout's Drugstore was a barbershop, an even better place for men to share news. Women had their haunts. Several small corner grocers provided the basics and opportunities to meet and visit: Boehm's Grocery at the corner of Washington and Belleview; Davis Grocery at Addison and New York; and Minker Grocery at Belleview and Ohio cater-corner from Hawthorne School. There were two family physicians in the area, a luxury by today's standards, and an open-air picture show called the Eureka in back of a pharmacy on Addison. Other businesses were interspersed between well-to-do homes scattered along Washington Street between Belmont and Warman.[69]

Men could gather in the local bars for beer. Bars might also serve food, and families could come for a meal. There was no shortage of choices. One of the most popular, a bar and restaurant, was the Belmont Lunch Room (renamed the "Workingman's Friend" during the Depression) at the intersection of Belmont and Turner in the northeast corner of the neighborhood next to the B & O Railroad. Founded in 1918 this small family-owned eatery and pub served simple meals and the popular Indiana brewed Champagne Velvet beer to the local industrial laborers and residents from the area.[70]

Sports

Sports dominated much of the social life of the Hawthorne community, as it did for the Westside and the city generally. One example illustrates how deeply basketball was embedded in community life. In 1920 the Washington Street United Methodists began building a new church. After the basement was completed, the congregation began meeting in the finished basement area. Still surrounded by the confusion and the demands of unfinished construction, they decided to organize a basketball team. To be a member of the team you had to attend Mrs. Andrew Cossell's Sunday School class! The team excelled, traveling the southern part of the state and winning eighty percent of their games.[71] Similarly, almost every church, school, factory, civic organization, and business in the neighborhood either organized a sports team of some kind, usually basketball, or committed themselves to sponsoring one.

This love of basketball continued to flower, not only in the churches and the schools but also in the Hawthorne Center. Once the new Hawthorne Community Center gymnasium was built it became possible to give full expression to that obsession by providing a regular opportunity for competition that always promised the possibility of a comeback next year for the losers. By the early thirties as many as eighteen basketball teams used the Hawthorne Center gym regularly.

George Washington High School, too, fed that love of sports. After it had been in operation for over a decade their basketball team was already making a name for itself. In 1935, and again in 1937, Washington's *Continentals* defeated principal rivals Broad Ripple, Manual, and Shortridge to win the City High School Basketball Championship, euphoric moments for Hawthorne and the whole Westside.[72] Conversation about the current sports activities was constant---from the workplace, to the barbershop, to local church suppers and the family dinner table---and of course was reflected in the local and city newspapers.

Not All Rosy

Life in Hawthorne between the wars was not quite the idyllic place sometimes recalled in popular memory. For instance, Robert Howard remembered that for an Irish boy living in the westside of Indianapolis it was "a tough place to live." There were gangs organized by neighborhood. "There also was the necessity of earning the right to belong to a gang, for if you lived in Mt. Jackson, as I did, you couldn't venture into other neighborhoods unless you went in force."

There were attractions that lured young folk beyond Hawthorne if their parents allowed, although many did not. Rhodius Park south of the tracks boasted the only municipal swimming pool on the Westside, an obvious attraction for youth. It also held Saturday night amateur boxing for those boys who were more daring. For this reason Rhodius Park was considered neutral territory by the gangs, and the boxing ring a place for peaceful competition between the gangs, a relief valve for tensions it was hoped. But anywhere in The Valley, "You were fair game for a fight going and coming."[73] Former Indianapolis Mayor Charles Boswell [Mayor of Indianapolis 1959-62] recalled of the Westside where he grew up during this period, "We got along with each other on all the days except when we fought; the fighting didn't take place more than five to six days a week," perhaps reflecting a bit of truth in his humorous exaggeration.[74]

Haughville north of the tracks was also perceived as territory to be entered cautiously by Hawthorne youth. Those residents came from different cultures, often spoke a different language, went to different schools (until GWHS opened), and did not take kindly to strangers wandering into their neighborhood. The pre-war conflict between St. Anthony's "Irish congregation" and Haughville's eastern European (Slovene) peoples was carried forward into the 1920s. Even dating across these boundaries was discouraged. Residents west of the White River were all aware of the boundaries.

> Young men from St. Anthony's walking north of Michigan Street or young Holy Trinity men penetrating St. Anthony territory [Hawthorne] frequently found themselves unwelcome. This lack of hospitality usually took the form of being accosted and subjected to physical violence (fancy way of saying that they stopped you and beat you up).[75]

In the post-war anti-immigrant "100% American" environment, both young people and adults from Hawthorne sometimes dismissed residents north of the tracks as "hunkies," an ethnic slur against laborers from Central Europe, a label that most did not understand but which was nonetheless good enough reason for a fight. What mattered was that they were different! To the south was "the Valley," with its own history and sense of identity. To the east the neighborhood of Stringtown was an older but much poorer neighborhood than Hawthorne, and at that time considered by many Hawthorne parents as unsafe for their children, a belief that further clarified neighborhood boundaries and lingered on into the post-World War II years.[76]

There were also differences within Hawthorne from time to time. An example was the appearance of the Ku Klux Klan in Indianapolis. The Klan had come to Indianapolis in early 1921 hoisting the banner of "100% Americanism." In the atmosphere of intense patriotism that remained from the war, it quickly took root in the city's political establishment, and in the neighborhoods.[77] The most common explanation offered for Klan popularity whenever it is discussed --- deep racial and religious bigotry against Blacks, Jews, and Catholics---was only part of the reason driving its success in Indianapolis. Certainly those prejudices were present, and recent immigrants were an easy target for the Klan. But the appeal of the Klan to others in the community, the hook which might have also pulled in the hard-working church-going protestants, had to do with the part of the Klan's message that included a focus on "law enforcement, motherhood, virtue, patriotism, and temperance" and "charitable activity."[78] These were the same concerns preached from the pulpits of both Catholic and Protestant churches pretty much everywhere at this time, as well as from the many social and religious societies.

The Klan in Indianapolis also strongly supported making much needed improvements in the public schools, and pressed for the building of new schools. In the Westside at that time local leaders were trying desperately to get the city to build a high school in the area to avoid their high school students having to travel all the way into the city. In addition to a range of damaging prejudices, then, the Klan message also included popular concerns.

Public wearing of the symbolic Klan robe and masked hood by both men and women accompanied special occasions in the neighborhood and ensured a degree of conflict.[79] One incident illustrates the way in which those tensions manifested publicly in Hawthorne. The Rev. C. G. Baker, a Disciples of Christ pastor at West Park Christian Church at this time, editor/publisher of the (then named) *West Side Christian Messenger* and highly respected civic leader, had been outspoken against the Klan from the start. *The Fiery Cross,* the Klan's official publication, was in fact located in the 300 block of N. Addison just north of Rev. C. G. Baker's own house from which the *Messenger* was being composed and distributed. Baker had used his paper to fight the intolerance generated by the movement.[80] Occasionally voicing his views from the pulpit had led to disagreements with some church members who supported the Klan.

One Sunday morning in 1923 several members showed up at his church service in full Klan regalia, a Klan practice in other churches in the city at this time.[81] His immediate instruction to the ushers to escort the Klansmen out of the sanctuary created a strong reaction within the congregation. He resigned soon after.[82] Rev. Baker never spoke publicly about that incident, or about his resignation from the pastorate that followed the incident. He never served again as pastor in any church, though he remained active in another larger church in the city. At that time he also, without explanation, changed the title of his newspaper from *West Side Christian Messenger* to *West Side Messenger,* leaving out the word "Christian."

The same year that Rev. Baker left the pulpit, in 1923, he became one of the founders and the first Executive Director of the Hawthorne Community Center, a position that he held for a quarter century. He remained living in the neighborhood where he and his family had become deeply involved in the life of the community, and continued to be a major leader for progressive change in Hawthorne and the Westside until his death at 92.[83]

In the 1930s the Great Depression hit this working-class neighborhood hard, as it did everywhere. Layoffs mounted and several major employers closed their doors. The *West Side Messenger,* as with all businesses, had to let some of their employees go and reduce the salaries of others. But a strong community spirit remained. The churches, the schools, and the Community Center all cooperated to ease the hardships wherever possible, and to make the Center's mortgage payments and maintain its facilities. They found creative ways to try to make up for the loss of usual sources of income: church suppers and weekly luncheons in church basements, fish fries in the park at the intersection of Belleview and Washington, shows and plays charging a minimum admission.[84] St. Anthony's even began charging "pew rent" for families who wished to reserve a pew, and they encouraged all to adopt this practice in order to help the church meet its fiscal demands.[85] Some families were forced to move further west or south into the country in order to farm.[86] In some areas the physical state of housing declined noticeably for lack of regular maintenance. Remarkably George Washington High School (GWHS) managed to complete a much-needed new addition during these difficult years.[87] Nothing in the school newspaper (*The Surveyor*) suggested a serious cutback in activities or the community's support for them. Nor did the *West Side Messenger* focus unduly on the economic hardships of the time.

The GWHS community, which included Hawthorne and surrounding neighborhoods, was not without its challenges between the wars. From its founding it had to deal with the cultural and language differences of a diverse Westside: Irish, Appalachian, several East European groups (mainly Slovenes). Cloyd Julian, a GWHS teacher and coach from 1937 to 1960, recalled his first years at Washington.

> At that time [1930s] this was the foreign section of the city. They were largely Slavs and worked in the steel mills. When I came here in '37, many of the students' parents didn't even speak English, but the children went on to be professional people like doctors, lawyers, dentists and businessmen.[88]

He acknowledged that the neighborhoods continued to have their own distinctive personalities. There were sometimes fights between young folk, though not often he added, and they took place in the neighborhoods, not in school. "They were all proud of their own communities," and quick to let you know about it, said Julian. It is clear from looking at Washington's academic curriculum and extra-curricular activities, and the athletics program, and reading *The Surveyor*, that GWHS teachers, coaches and administrators ran a tight ship regarding expectations and discipline. It is easy to imagine that students were simply too busy to get into trouble.

Naming the Neighborhood

When the Indianapolis Land & Improvement Company purchased the west half of what is today Hawthorne neighborhood from the Flack farm and laid out 380 residential lots for sale in 1901-02, they entitled the plot map "West Park Sub-division." That name stuck. The first Protestant church built soon after in this new development, completed in1905, chose the name West Park Christian Church. The developer Trotter & Henry Company purchased the eastern half of the farm a few years later, but the name "West Park" remained for this emerging neighborhood in its very early years.

The neighborhood's name of "Hawthorne" appeared gradually. Nathanial Hawthorne School (School #50), the Hawthorne Library, and Hawthorne Community Center were built so close to one another and generated such a high level of involvement and activity in the neighborhood that the name began to take hold naturally. The association that was formed in the early 1920s to purchase a strip of Flack's farm and to consider building a community center was first named the "West Park Social Service Association," but it changed almost immediately to the "Hawthorne Social Service Association." From that point on, the name "Hawthorne" began to spread slowly, competing with and then gradually replacing the name "West Park." Hawthorne's identity as an independent neighborhood evolved very naturally during these interwar years.

* * *

Between the wars Hawthorne matured into a stable, relatively homogenous White working class community. The neighborhood was small enough that everything was within easy walking distance, and too small for divisive groups of like-minded folk to isolate themselves. The membership of St. Anthony's Catholic Church and the several protestant churches was scattered throughout the neighborhood making religious enclaves difficult.[89] Adults and children encountered one another at the public library, at church, in the stores, in school, at sports events, and at the Center's frequent club meetings (of which there were many), and at other social organizations and events. These organizations provided the institutional framework necessary for a vital civic life. It was this complex web of overlapping social networks reaching out into a small geographical area and drawing people in on many different levels that created a real *community*. The *West Side Messenger* fed the spirit of community by reporting everything from births, weddings and deaths to the least important happenings.

All three of the named "Hawthorne" properties were well-known public landmarks and located within a few yards of one another—Hawthorne Center, Hawthorne Library, and Hawthorne School (#50). When you set foot on one it was a little like walking onto a campus. It comprised what one newspaper article in the 1930s called "Hawthorne University" because "they are grouped together and work together, co-operating with each other in various projects."[90] Their specialties complemented each other. Their administrative activities sometimes overlapped, and they all focused upon the same clientele.

Between the end of this interwar period and the 1950s, the names Mt. Jackson and West Park gave way to "Hawthorne." A 1962 *Indianapolis Times* article entitled "Hawthorne: Homey Area On West Side," sums up that transformation.

> Here is the neighborhood known as Hawthorne, originally named after the school, now more firmly identified by the community center. It is the middle of the old West Side, bordered on the north by Haughville and on the south by West Indianapolis. There was a time when more people would have known this general area as Mt. Jackson, which was the original name of the neighborhood school. But the name, like the once incorporated community of Mt. Jackson, belongs to the past.[91]

Chapter 8

Hawthorne in the Post War Years

During World War II the location of Indianapolis as a railroad crossroads brought much activity to the city, including over six million military personnel by one estimate, and the demands for supplies and services that came with it.[92] Just as throughout the country, everyone in Indianapolis participated in the rationing of food and other essential products, as well as fire drills, practice air raids, blackouts, preparation of bandages for the troops, special drives to collect products for the war effort, the purchase of war bonds, and a host of other war-related efforts. Students at George Washington High School joined efforts to support the war by organizing drives for scrap metal, food stuffs and clothing, and raised thousands of dollars worth of bonds and stamps. Eighteen hundred GWHS students and former students, and one faculty member, actually served in World War II. Ninety-five from the school that had responded to the call died in the war. The school honored them, listing their names on a permanent memorial hanging inside the entrance hallway under the epitaph "THOSE WHO GAVE ALL."[93]

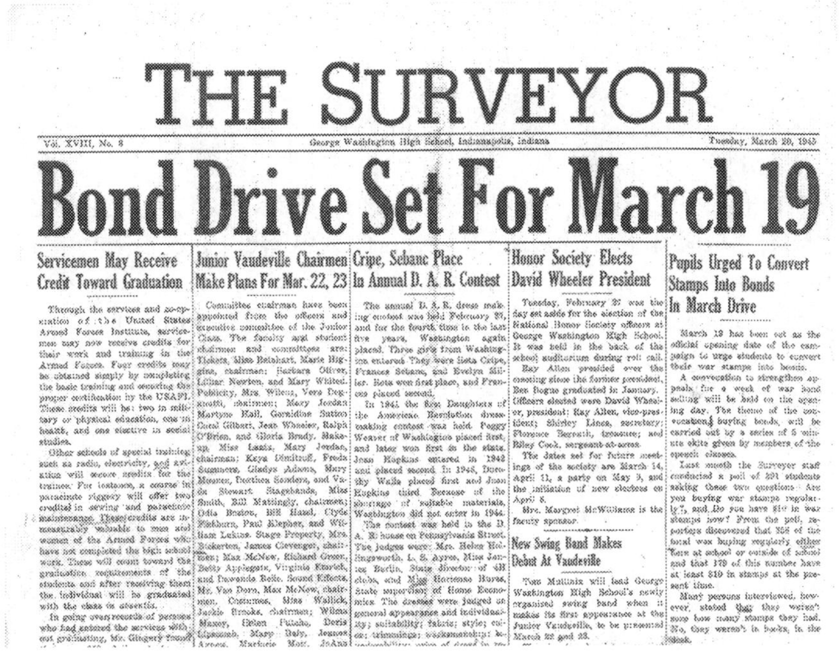

THE SURVEYOR

Vol. XVIII, No. 8 — George Washington High School, Indianapolis, Indiana — Tuesday, March 20, 1945

Bond Drive Set For March 19

Servicemen May Receive Credit Toward Graduation

Junior Vaudeville Chairmen Make Plans For Mar. 22, 23

Cripe, Sebanc Place In Annual D. A. R. Contest

Honor Society Elects David Wheeler President

Pupils Urged To Convert Stamps Into Bonds In March Drive

Figure 17 George Washington High School Student Newspaper

The Surveyor, March 20, 1945

The war brought full employment, and a tsunami of changes. In general, during the war the city became "bigger, more modern, more industrial, more diverse, and perhaps more cosmopolitan and open."[94] The post-war years in Indianapolis experienced a population explosion, and a housing boom brought on by post-war optimism and a flood of returning veterans who needed affordable homes immediately. One consequence of this wave of change was a reshaping of the city's social and economic geography as many families abandoned their neighborhoods in the city and moved out to the suburbs, setting off a slow spiral of decline in some of the older neighborhoods.

That decline was not immediately evident in Hawthorne neighborhood. Anyone visiting the Hawthorne community in the 1950s would have experienced a thriving and confident community. Life in Hawthorne in the late 40s and 50s seemed more of a continuation of pre-war patterns, only better. They had survived the Depression and the war. And Hawthorne's social and economic environment was anchored by a wide range of institutions, all of them healthy and looking confidently to the future.

In 1949 the Hawthorne Center commemorated its 25th year by making the final mortgage payment on the property and marking that milestone with a big celebration and public burning of the mortgage.[95] By 1949 membership in the Hawthorne Center had reached new highs catering to over 112 different local groups and clubs, offering the community virtually every type of recreation, and hosting 343 meetings a month attended by more than 8,044 people! It held a Free Kindergarten every morning, and in the afternoon meetings of "Girl Scouts, Boy Scouts, Camp Fire Girls, Blue Birds, Bear Club and numerous other groups, as well as 5 leagues of basketball, composed of 36 teams," twenty-two of which were sponsored by the Center itself.[96] The quarter century of the Center's existence was indeed cause for celebration. It had assumed an important role in leadership of the community and surrounding neighborhoods through years of steady growth and success. As they celebrated their 25th anniversary there was every indication that the community was on solid footing and would continue to prosper.

Membership in the neighborhood churches also expanded in the 1950s, as it did throughout the city.[97] West Park Christian Church membership peaked in 1955, the year of its 50th anniversary. Its programs flourished and fed the strong belief, expressed in its Golden Jubilee publication and felt throughout the neighborhood, that "there is more reason to hope for a great future than there has ever been before."[98] St. Anthony's membership, too, reached its height one year later in 1956.[99]

Figure 18 West Park Christian Church Congregation in 1946

A number of businesses had taken root along Washington Street in the decades before World War II creating a solid commercial strip from east of Belmont west to Warman and absorbing the village of Mt. Jackson. Now, in the post-war years, this strip was buzzing with new prosperity. It was "like a little town," remembers Cloyd Julian, the principal of George Washington High School during those years.[100] The neighborhood schools provided another layer of the community's energy. Three grade schools served the area, IPS School #50 (Hawthorne School) and St. Anthony's Parochial School, and IPS School #30 in Stringtown. School and after-school programs in Hawthorne flourished. A growing population of young students went on to Washington High School where they competed successfully with other schools in the city in academics and the arts and in sports.

GWHS brought together the young people and their families from the whole Westside providing a unifying influence. The school cooperated with all three community centers that served the Westside area: Hawthorne, Christamore, and Mary Riggs; and their relationships were cordial.[101] Neighborhood differences and boundaries remained meaningful and clear in residents' minds. But the differences were moderated by the wide range of shared classroom experiences and extracurricular activities, as well as by loyalty to the school.

CHAPTER 9

Changes in the Neighborhood: Harbingers?

Most residents of the Westside in the post-war years expected life would return to the pre-war norm.The abundant activities of institutions they had been developing so successfully between the wars reinforced that expectation. Yet there were hints that this stability might not hold.

Changing Leadership

In Hawthorne the large gathering in 1949 at the Hawthorne Center commemorating its 25th year was clearly a cause for celebration. This evening was also an occasion for honoring the founding father of the Hawthorne Center and a principal community leader, Rev. Clarence G. Baker, who was now retiring after 25 years as the Center's Director.[102] Within a week, Mr. Royster, local businessman and the first president of the Center's Board of Directors, also retired. A pillar of the business community and a close friend of Rev. Baker, Royster had been deeply involved in the initiatives and programs of the Hawthorne Center and the neighborhood. His leaving at the same time as Baker left a leadership vacuum. Less than two years later in 1951 Walter Gingery, another recognized leader in the community and

Washington High School's first principal, retired after almost 25 years in that position. Three of the community's outstanding longtime community leaders were no longer at the helm, and others of that generation soon followed. It was the beginning of generational turnover. The character of the community Baker, Gingery, Royster and other leaders of their generation had helped to shape between the wars was shifting. What kind of impact that might have was not yet considered by the new leadership. In the case of the Hawthorne Center, almost two decades later a 1966 Center "Program Report" reflected back more clearly on this period of leadership turnover as a significant change in the Center's focus.

> Although the primary function of the Hawthorne Social Service Association has always been the maintenance of a community center, neighborhood planning and organization as practiced by Rev. C. G. Baker, the founder and original director, was a vital dynamic aspect of the program. During the years following Rev. Baker's retirement, the neighborhood organization function declined in importance, and little emphasis was placed on social service programs. The primary function of Hawthorne House was it's recreational program, although limited informal counseling was carried out by various staff members . . . this function [focusing on recreation] continued until December 31, 1965, with the approval of the Board of Directors.[103]

It appears that the founders generation, represented by the neighborhood's women and men seen in the photograph of the first Hawthorne Community Association (See fig. 11), had a broad view of the health of the community that extended beyond recreation. This current emphasis upon recreation and social activities rather than addressing the basic needs of the community reflected the Center's confidence that those were the most needed programs at the time. But this confidence only lasted until the 1960s when the economic and social effects of serious urban change throughout the city finally began to penetrate Hawthorne forcing a reexamination of the Center's direction and policies.

Hawthorne Library Closes

One event that was recognized at the time by Hawthorne residents as threatening to the community was the 1955 closing of the Hawthorne Library, one of the oldest institutions in the community. Founded in 1911 as a Carnegie library, its solid facade symbolized permanence and stability, and it provided just that. It had been a part of the daily life of three generations of young folk that had grown up attending a range of community meetings and events in that building: social, educational, and sports. It had offered them a chance to meet away from the watchful eyes of parents, and of course the opportunity to draw on their book collection.

Figure 19 Former Hawthorne Library

Located across the street from the Community Center, right behind School #50 (Hawthorne School), and a short walk to the churches and to Washington High School, this prominent building was quite literally a geographic center of the neighborhood. Residents simply could not imagine its closing. Yet the library's circulation numbers had been the lowest in the city's system for several years, partly because they were located very near two other newer libraries in neighborhoods to the north and south of them, and partly because the schools had now developed their own libraries. Hawthorne was logically the first to be cut.[104]

Despite the statistics arguing for closure, however, it simply felt to residents like an unjust and ill-founded decision by the authorities. So the outpouring of protests from the community was understandable. Despite many meetings with city officials and a petition to the Board of School Commissioners, this symbolic pillar of the community was nevertheless closed for good on September 1, 1955.[105] It was a shot across the bow in terms of the changes that took place in the years that followed. As it turned out, however, this resource was not totally lost to the community. Ultimately it became an annex to the Hawthorne Center.

Changes in Popular Culture

Change in the community's leadership and a later shift in the Center's focus towards more social services coincided with a larger theme affecting the community, the front edge of a social and cultural shift (albeit an introductory phase) that affected Hawthorne no less than its neighbors and the rest of the country. While 1950s parents were sitting in front of their new black and white TV screens watching a range of sports events and game shows, Marshall Matt Dillon in "Gun Smoke," Jackie Gleason on "The Honeymooners," or the comedian Milton Berle, their kids were watching American Bandstand after school, experimenting with the jitter bug at social gatherings, listening on the radio or their 45 record players to the latest Rock and Roll hits, and making a transition from the Mickey Mouse Club to the new sounds and shakes of Elvis Presley, Jerry Lee Lewis, and to Little Richard, the first Black singer to make the breakthrough into White popular culture.

As everywhere in the fifties, the Rock and Roll revolution brought changes to Hawthorne in young folk's music tastes, hairstyles and dress, and a kind of behavior which began to challenge traditional norms. Adults in Hawthorne tried to influence the changing culture of their young people, an uphill battle at best. The Hawthorne Center, where adult leaders had daily contact with the youth, became a voice for the enforcement of the community's older standards against the new more liberal behaviors.

This all seems so innocent in retrospect, but it was taken very seriously at the time. This perceived threat was discussed at the Center's Board meetings ("What is happening to our young people?"). It was expected that office staff, supervisors, and coaches should serve as role models and redirect the young people towards more appropriate behavior and dress. In response to this challenge they created the Hawthorne Teen Service Club, as well as a mimeographed newsletter for teens called "Hawthorne Happenings" hoping to influence the youth. In one 1960 issue the volunteer club sponsor, Marie Kenley (later to become the Hawthorne Center's Director) included an open letter to members encouraging them to dress appropriately for an upcoming dance sponsored by the Center!

> Teen advertising has more sway with the teens than any other form of advertising . . . As for wearing dresses, it is a must for the Service Club. You are an example, at all times and if you set the right example, others will follow you . . . Learning what to wear is a part of growing up. It takes more time for some of us to mature than others . . . Remember this is our Center, not your Center nor my Center. Hawthorne was founded as an idea of the community and we are all a part of this image, from Lassies to Basketball.[106]

Commenting on dress later in the same issue, the student president of the Hawthorne Teen Service Club voiced the adult concerns to her peers: "So come on style conscious gals, lets do away with the beatnik look and go back to being little girls again."

It is helpful to remember that much more dire changes were taking place throughout the country and beyond that likely heightened adults' unrest in Hawthorne as elsewhere: the rise of the Soviet Communist Bloc in Europe, the communist victory in China in 1949, and the Korean War of the early 1950s only five years after the end of World War II, and more. The U. S. had come out of its isolation, and this deluge of global events reminded older folk that the world had changed. And in this country, the Cold War anti-communist reactions, in particular the McCarthy hearings of the mid-fifties, heightened that sense of threat. The fear of nuclear war caused schools to plan Duck-and-Cover drills that sent students hiding under their desks. Added to this, a series of events fed the Civil Rights movement in the middle of the decade and threatened the privileged status quo of White Americans: the 1954 Brown vs Board of Education (declaring school segregation unconstitutional); the Emmett Till lynching (1955); the 1955-6 Montgomery Bus Boycott, the first "sit-ins"; and many other related developments that were making daily newspaper headlines, and now beginning to appear on black and white television.

But to the teenagers growing up in the 1950s, the changes in music tastes and dress and the social behavior that accompanied them seemed more important. As elsewhere, parental attempts to discourage youth from the popular influences of this decade were largely ineffective, even though these influences paled by comparison with what followed in the 1960s and 70s—the Beatles, long-hair on males, the Hippies, LSD, the mini-skirt, more violent civil rights clashes, assassinations of national leaders, the Vietnam War, and the frequent protests and counter protests that accompanied these developments.

In the middle of the neighborhood's social and cultural changes, fire struck the Hawthorne Center in April 1966, and again in 1975. The first fire only damaged the roof. The second destroyed about three-quarters of the building, including many of their records and other important papers. Local fund-raising and supporting grants from organizations in Indianapolis restored the Center quickly demonstrating continued strong community and city support for the valuable work they were doing.

CHAPTER 10

Decades of Struggle

After World War II some Westside residents began to move to the outer suburbs that were sprouting further west and north where they found better jobs and affordable and newer housing. So began a pace of change in this area that increased without relief in the decades that followed. Hawthorne was the last of the three neighborhoods in the Westside to experience this wave of changes. But it, too, eventually felt its full force. Increasingly during this period we are forced to observe developments from the perspective of the Hawthorne Center as many of the other institutions in the neighborhood weakened and disappeared.

"Newcomers" and the Center's Changed Mission

As flight to the suburbs made cheap housing available in Hawthorne and Stringtown, White Protestants from the Appalachian areas of Tennessee and Kentucky and from southern Indiana took advantage of it as they sought jobs in local industries. African Americans from the South also began moving into Haughville for similar reasons, cheap housing and access to jobs locally. Residents of Hawthorne had initially observed this population turnover in surrounding neighborhoods but hadn't initially experience it themselves. By the late sixties, however, these changes were finally beginning to affect Hawthorne as well.

Each family that moved out of Hawthorne carried with it the personal commitments and the financial resources that had helped to build up and support the neighborhood from its beginning. Families with much lower household incomes and no such ties to the community replaced them. "Newcomers" they were now referred to in the Center's reports. Until now the social environment of Hawthorne had been strongly influenced by the founders generation. Many of the older residents were still around, but the social and economic character of the community they helped to build had begun to change. The local resources available for maintaining a stable and viable community, once taken for granted, now began to disappear—contributions to churches, spending in local businesses, charitable giving, various forms of support for school and community-wide projects, volunteers, to mention the most obvious.

For example, beginning in the late 50s and 60s St. Anthony's parochial school saw a dramatic rise in the number of "parents who would not, or could not, pay for school supplies or tuition." The number of school supplies that had to be given free to families almost doubled between 1958-9 and again in 1961-2. In the 1961-62 year, thirty percent of the school children did not pay their tuition, a problem that increasingly plagued the school and the congregation.[107] The Hawthorne Center, too, was beginning to experience this new reality---a neighborhood with an increasing number of newcomers who did not so easily assimilate into the existing social networks, or make the same economic or personal contributions to support the Center's work.

Other parts of the city were experiencing similar kinds of change. Because neighborhoods lacked the funds and personnel to address these growing problems themselves city leaders organized the Indianapolis Settlements, Inc. (ISI) in 1959 to encourage a common approach to dealing with the economic and social needs of the neighborhoods. It was the job of ISI's new Director, Mrs. Alfred Dobrof, to help the neighborhoods organize themselves for the challenge. Hawthorne was the first neighborhood on the Westside visited by Mrs. Dobrof.

In December 1959 the Hawthorne Center Board approved a plan to give her $500 to conduct a survey and report on Hawthorne's needs. The survey was completed during the next four months, and she produced a written report that became an important turning point in Hawthorne's approach to serving the community. She reported on the findings in a formal address to the annual Board of Directors meeting of the Hawthorne Social Services Association in May 1960.[108] It was Hawthorne's first professional and comprehensive assessment of the community's problems. Her speech was transformative.

Mrs. Dobrof, like one of the Center's founders and first Executive Director Rev. Baker almost four decades earlier, was a New Deal Democrat devoted to caring for members of the struggling underclass. In an effort to help Hawthorne's leaders put their newcomers into perspective, Dobrof reminded them of the waves of European immigrants a half century earlier, nationally as well as locally, that had given rise to the Settlement House movement, and of the more recent influx to the Westside of Blacks from the south and Whites from Appalachia. Clearly she was reminding them that immigration was nothing new on the Westside, and that many of those present had likely come out of an immigrant past and had needed similar help.

Ms. Dobrof's long speech to the Center focusing on the problems identified by her survey gave context and confirmation to what the Center and other community leaders had already begun to observe, "the presence of a number of [new] families who do not yet feel a part of the neighborhood and look to Hawthorne Center to help them in their adjustment to their new community."

> In this neighborhood, for example, you ministers and you who are the leaders of your churches are already feeling the loss of some of the families who were pillars of support in your churches . . . and at the same time are aware of the tremendous challenge which the newcomers to the neighborhood present to you . . . All of these problems of the city life are present here, in this neighborhood . . . and all call for the efforts of all of us.[109]

She recommended the organization of a "Newcomers Club," which the Center started soon after.

From this point on, with Dobrof's strong encouragement, Hawthorne's discussion of its challenges became more public and helped to lead the Center in a marked shift away from it's primary focus on recreational activities. They continued to serve the young folk through social and recreational programs, an important service. Now, however, they were also drawn to serving more basic needs of the newcomers, as well as the needs of the older residents many of whose younger family members had left the neighborhood for a new life in the suburbs.

Dobrof's arguments and proposals were also successful in helping to extend the Center's services beyond its traditional boundaries into neighboring Stringtown where the needs were much more immediate. The Hawthorne Center's Board Minutes of September 1962 indicated their intention: "It was suggested that thought be given to ways Hawthorne House could make its services more available to children living east of Belmont in the School #30 district [Stringtown]."[110]

Since the 1930s, Stringtown had sought to provide social services to its residents through a Neighborhood Association, but it lacked a community center such as both Hawthorne and Haughville had. Nor did they have other institutions in their neighborhood that were able to provide such continuing services. At that time Christamore House in Haughville was overwhelmed by the challenges of their changing populations and unable to help, leaving Hawthorne to respond. At it's annual Board of Directors meeting in 1964, the Hawthorne Social Service Association voted to join the Indianapolis Settlements, Inc., thereby formally aligning itself with the first large citywide effort to deal with the problems of changing neighborhoods. And in 1966 the Hawthorne Center's Program Report announced a Stringtown initiative.

> It was felt that a pilot project in the Stringtown
> neighborhood should be started in September, 1966,
> on a 3-month trial basis. The immediate goals of this
> project would be to serve 100 children (primarily
> girls) in small-group recreation programs, and 100

adults in a referral-consultation (primarily as a sounding-board) program.[111]

This new expanded responsibility beyond its traditional boundaries became a regular part of the Center's program for several years.

Changes in the Family

In the sixties and seventies other challenges were becoming apparent in Hawthorne, such as the changing socio-economic character of the neighborhood reflected in both the makeup of the family and in religious behavior. Mounting divorce rates produced single parent families headed by mothers. Many moms went to work leaving the home without an adult during the day. A 1968 survey of the Hawthorne area noted that there were already 89 single parent families, and 214 families with both parents working.[112]

As those numbers continued to rise, changing family roles were also creating problems. And once again the Hawthorne Center responded. Looking back on this period from an early 2000s perspective, the Center Director recalled some of these problems.

> At one time in our program almost twenty percent of the children [did not have a parent at home during the day] . . . That was during the women's liberation period that women decided they didn't want to be mothers anymore and they left, and so fathers were raising their children . . . We kind of had to step in and be surrogate mothers for some of these fathers who really wanted to do a good job but who really didn't know how to deal with it, didn't know how to treat head lice, didn't know what chicken pox looked like . . . So we kind of had to change to that nurturing role and step in for that.[113]

As time went on, the makeup of families changed placing additional pressure on the expanding list of needs for the community.

> We'd gone from nuclear families to single parent mother families, to single parent mother and father families, to the last 10 or 15 years probably more grandparents raising their children, or three generations living in the same household—parents, children, and grandchildren.[114]

Economic conditions continued to worsen and community institutions had to adjust their programs to accommodate the new conditions. Volunteer mothers, once vital to the neighborhood's social networks and to most community organizations and activities, began to disappear. Church organizations, community center activities, the schools, all had to begin to explore ways of doing without that previous available volunteer labor and leadership. Newcomers with different loyalties and behaviors replaced the families leaving the neighborhood. Unlike the pre-war residents, for instance, the newcomers often were not churchgoers and so did not become a part of those supportive networks.

Plant and Business Closings

At the same time significant economic changes were taking place throughout Indianapolis as it readjusted to the post-war situation---the decline of the manufacturing sector and a shift to more service-oriented industries, and the movement of populations to the suburbs. As these trends reached the Westside stability and prosperity couldn't hold. Plant closings and growing unemployment was the first of these changes to impact the Hawthorne neighborhood.

Two of the largest employers began closing their doors within two years of one another: the local Link-Belt plant in 1959, and National Malleable and Steel Casting Company in 1962. Four years later the large Kingan Company also closed. For years these industries had hired workers from all of the neighborhoods on the Westside, significantly from Hawthorne. These companies had grown up along with the area, had helped to create it, and were a vital part of the social as well as the economic fabric. They had provided a steady income and a familiar workplace and routine that lent a degree of predictability and stability to the neighborhood. Many of their employees could actually walk to their jobs. One resident who grew up in Hawthorne during these years remembers what the area around nearby Link-Belt was like before and after the closings.

> I can remember when Link-Belt ran three shifts a day, literally ran twenty-four hours. And then they kept cutting back and cutting back, and then cut back to just one shift . . .You used to go by at 4 o'clock in the afternoon and you couldn't get up and down Belmont between Washington and Morris because hundreds of people were leaving . . . [After the plant closings] the community became more transient because there wasn't that stability of working in your neighborhood.[115]

These closings, the first of many, brought disruption and uncertainty to the area and triggered a chain reaction of responses, first in Haughville and Stringtown, and later in Hawthorne.

At first, even as these closings took place, normal routines and activities continued in the Hawthorne Center, and in the churches and schools. But a once confident self-supporting community now began to worry over the changes and how to respond. Loss of jobs forced families to leave the neighborhood in search of work. Those who remained often took less desirable jobs with less pay, often much further away from their homes.

Other significant economic changes were taking place in the area at the same time. Chain stores moved into the Westside driving older and smaller competitors out of business (Krogers on Michigan Street, Burger Chef on Washington Street, Marsh grocery store on Rockville Road and Lynhurst, to name a few). Construction of Eagledale Mall, one of the first malls in Indianapolis, built northwest of Hawthorne in the suburbs, enticed customers away from the smaller local businesses. The construction of I-465 made it easier for everyone to go somewhere else for their purchases, and they did. This new competition combined with the increasing unemployment in the area to undermine the local economy. Little by little, starting in the seventies, the small independent businesses in Hawthorne began to close for lack of customers: the corner grocers and drug stores, and small businesses such as Peppy's Grill, Benny's Bakery, and the Standard Grocery. Ultimately, despite protests and many meetings, even the two banks in the area, Indiana National Bank and Merchants National Bank, also closed. Merchants National was the last, in 1989, marked by public protests.[116]

Hawthorne Clings to Its Identity

Despite the plant closings that began in 1959 and the rising unemployment affecting all of the Westside, many Hawthorne residents still clung tenaciously to their neighborhood identity as distinct from surrounding neighborhoods, better off than their neighbors, even as they were beginning to sense that the foundations of that identity might be shifting beneath them.

In 1962 one of the older residents of Hawthorne, Mrs. Alyce Eddy, captured that feeling long held by Hawthorne residents that their little community was both different and better off than their neighbors. She had lived all of her life in Hawthorne and still lived in the house at 70 N. Addison built by her father in 1902 when she was a baby. With such a long-standing residency, her comments on the neighborhood are particularly interesting.

> The unusual thing is that [the neighborhood] has stayed about the same. The people are in the same income group and the majority of them own their own homes . . . Hawthorne could not be considered a wealthy community, but it is probably better off economically than its neighbors. It is mainly residential one-family homes on tree-lined streets, owned by the families who lived in them.[117]

A 1965 Hawthorne Center internal "Report on Services and Programs" for the neighborhood revealed a similar optimism.

> This neighborhood is a Caucasian neighborhood, predominantly middle-aged, with a total population of 2905. The community is relatively stable, with many families having lived in the neighborhood over twenty years. There exists a strong, but unstructured, community spirit which is evidenced by the high level of property maintenance. Of the three neighborhoods in the Hawthorne community [area] this has the lowest number of serious problem areas.[118]

Those who grew up in the early sixties have fond memories of a daily routine during that period: one that included walking to school and going to the Hawthorne Center for after school programs; one filled with a strong school spirit nurtured by weekends of football and basketball games, frequent church suppers, and annual carnivals; one where most of the mothers did not work outside the home, were involved in the PTA, and volunteered in numerous community undertakings.[119] It had been a community with many layers of interwoven loyalties that produced a sense of stability. Most residents did not yet recognize the seriousness of the looming threats. And the statistics for Stringtown and Haughville, always much worse, validated in Center Report narratives that seemed to indicate that life in Hawthorne was not so bad after all!

A 1968 Hawthorne working paper for a self-study offered little more than a hint of change in the narrative portion of the report. It painted a pretty normal picture of life in the Hawthorne community. Small shops and stores along Washington Street provided all of the basic needs as they had always done. The three grade schools in the area, together with Washington High School, were still functioning. There were six active well-maintained churches in the area: Catholic, Presbyterian, Methodist, Christian, Free Methodist, and Baptist.[120]

In 1969 a large self-study by neighborhoods, supervised by the Indianapolis Settlements, Inc. (ISI), confirmed the perception of Hawthorne residents that they had always been a leader among the other neighborhoods, and more progressive than the others. Conditions were different in neighboring areas. Christamore House (Haughville) to its north now served a largely African-American neighborhood "characterized by poverty and racial tension, underemployment and unemployment, under achievement in school and high drop out rates." Stringtown, had a mostly low income Appalachian population with "poor crowded, dilapidated and deteriorating housing," and had recently experienced considerable low income migration from the south, and "junk yards and industry [that were] pushing farther and farther into the neighborhood." The downward spiral in the area continued, however. Eventually even folk in Hawthorne, "who have justifiably prided themselves that they have maintained a stable, solid, law abiding neighborhood in the face of many threats," began to acknowledge "serious challenges now as Public Housing Projects rise on the borders of the area and school redistricting is proposed."[121]

Selected Memories of GWHS in the 1960s

Any history of the Hawthorne neighborhood during these years of change has to acknowledge the importance of George Washington High School (GWHS) to the life of the community. Washington had always been noted for its excellence in academics and the arts, and impressive numbers of graduates achieved success in the professions. Drama productions, music performances, debates, news and literary publications enriched the life of the school. It was the sports teams, however, that frequently captured the enthusiasm and loyalty of Westside fans. The 1960s was GWHS's special time in sports, even as social and economic circumstances dramatically changed around them. Those who lived on the Westside during these years still recall the names of particular coaches and players, local heroes, several of whom went on to make names for themselves as players and as coaches at the state and national levels.[122]

Even before World War II Washington had established a reputation in basketball by winning the City High School Basketball Championship twice, once in 1935, and again in 1937. In the 1950s

Washington produced very good teams, but was beaten out by Crispus Attucks and Shortridge. That changed in the 1960s when Washington "ruled Indianapolis high school basketball" winning two state championships, in 1965 and again in 1969. They added two state titles in football, in 1966 and again in 1974 making it the only high school in Indiana to win two state titles in both basketball and football. "The Home of Champions" remained enshrined on a sign in front of the school and on their letterhead until the school closed in the nineties.[123] These were heady times for Washington's sports teams and for their fans, a welcome relief from the distressing news in other areas.

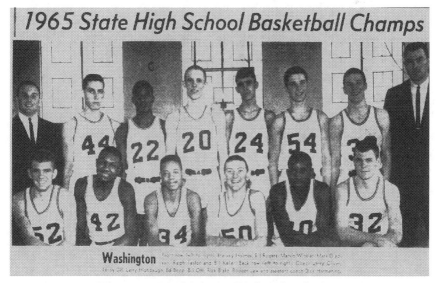

1965 State High School Basketball Champs

**Figure 20 Washington High School Wins
1965 State Basketball Champs**

The sixties was a decade in which changes taking place across the nation were ramping up and becoming an unavoidable part of public conversation everywhere. Television had now joined radio and newspapers to entertain as well as keep the public up-to-date on the latest Cold War crises, Civil Rights clashes, assassinations, and later in the decade protests against the Vietnam War.

The first of two important national issues that had an impact on GWHS was the Civil Rights movement. In 1964 President Johnson signed into law the landmark Civil Rights Act making it illegal to discriminate against persons on the basis of color, race, religion, sex, or national origin, or to deny them the right to vote or to have equal access to employment or public spaces. It further required that schools had to end segregation.

In the fifties and sixties a few African-American students had begun attending GWHS, most coming from nearby Haughville that had experienced an influx of African-Americans from the south after the war. Washington's first African-American teacher was hired in 1955, so Washington considered itself somewhat ahead of the mounting pressure from federal courts to integrate local schools. Still, there was no avoiding the impact of this issue on the local schools at all levels.

Most students who attended Washington High School in the early sixties were from White neighborhoods that had not been directly exposed to racial differences. But school was one place where actual interaction between races was now unavoidable and had to be dealt with on a regular basis. The sports programs played an important role in Washington's ability to manage potential racial conflict, partly because sports teams were leaders in efforts to integrate, and partly because they provided the school and the community with a unifying focus.

In 1965, just a few months after Congress passed the 1964 Civil Rights Act, Washington High School won the basketball State Championship. In Indiana very few things can trump that. The headlines in city's two largest newspapers announced the win. The *Indianapolis Star* read in large caps: WASHINGTON STATE CHAMP. Immediately beneath that was a second smaller headline, "U. S. Will Guard Alabama Marchers," followed by an article entitled "Thousands Mass in Selma As LBJ Sends Protection," next to a picture of Washington's jubilant players and coaches.[124] The *Indianapolis Times* had a similar format. Nothing could have captured the competing emotions of those troubled times so perfectly.

For Westside residents, the excitement of those playoffs and the celebrations of the final outcome left little room for focusing on other things. At that time only 8% of the students at Washington were African-American, but three of them played on the basketball team. By 1969 when Washington won its second State Championship, the number of African-American students at Washington had increased to about 40% of the student body with an equivalent increase on sports teams. Those intervening four years had seen a growing number of African-American students participating in student activities and organizations. Racial tensions at school had also increased.[125]

Bob Springer, the newly appointed football coach in 1962, sometimes had to deal with disgruntled sports fans. Years later a local sports writer recalled Springer's challenge.

> This [predominantly White team] made the "Westside Mafia"—some old Washington fans—very happy. But as more African-Americans entered the school, Springer could hear the jeers and ignorance from the fans. 'You are in love with the black athlete,' they yelled. 'What's wrong with you?' 'He can't play that position; he's black,' others screamed.[126]

Springer was a winning and a popular coach. He clearly had no problem with welcoming Blacks to the team, but he recognized the sensitivity of the issue and managed to minimize conflict. Springer recalled that he regularly "prayed to keep the races together at Washington High amid the boiling bigotry across the nation." The personal concern and respect he showed to every member of the team was obvious, and they returned that respect.

George McGinnis, Washington's most celebrated athlete at this time, followed the riots and marches going on in the nation and the ways in which Blacks like him were being treated. But at Washington, he remembered, "We were being treated with respect." Another Black athlete, Leonard Cannon, a member of the 1966 football championship team and a 1968 graduate, chose his words carefully: "We overlooked a lot of stuff. There were a few problems away from school, but it never entered the team. Even if we agreed or disagreed on those issues, it never got in the way of the team."

This focus on sports and their success during the sixties may have helped Washington dodge the more extreme kinds of racial clashes that happened in some other Indianapolis schools and across the country. The sports teams' discipline provided a model of behavior for students, and the team successes seemed, at least publically, to placate fans that were not happy with the integration of the teams. Much credit for Washington's "calming atmosphere of diversity" went to coach Springer and his staff, to the principal, Cloyd Julian, and to "the school's administration and teachers for being ahead of their time."[127] Julian ran a tight ship. Given his background experience as teacher and coach, and his earlier experience dealing with ethnic diversity at Washington, he was ideally suited to take over the job of principal in 1961, just in time to greet the school's largest freshman class (1000, a third of the school's total) and deal with the mounting challenges of the sixties.

In the late 1960s the country was also equally divided in their response to the Vietnam War. Vietnam was one small divided country, very distant and little understood by most of the public. The war was increasingly unpopular as the draft affected more and more young men, and as the casualties mounted. What constituted patriotism in this conflict was no longer uniformly agreed upon as in earlier wars, and there were few ways for Washington students to really involve themselves in the war effort as they had in World War II. Yet patriotism still ran high in the community and at school.

Young men had to register for the draft at 18, and some of the staff at Washington helped them do that. A few of the teachers also signed up. Male students now had to consider the possibility of being drafted and going to Vietnam. A sobering thought, particularly as the deaths of familiar Washington grads began to add up. Ivan Smith, the first Marine from Indiana to be killed, in 1965, was a 1964 Washington graduate from the neighborhood and known by a number of students still in school. His funeral at a church on Washington Street near the school brought the war home. Fifteen Washington graduates were killed in Vietnam through 1969, but likely more since the war lasted four more years. Some of those who made it back home safely were much changed by their experience and added to the mounting sense of disruption and loss within the local community.[128]

There were numerous major anti-war protests across the country in the late sixties. A few Washington teachers organized an anti-war

76

demonstration at the school. A few students, too, protested the Kent State killings and the war in the only ways available to them in school, such as refusing to stand for the National Anthem at convocations, or walking out of convocation in protest. Although those who did protest were occasionally disruptive, they were a small enough group that they could be easily dismissed as the "Wild Bunch."[129] But Washington's "Wild Bunch" and some of its teachers were in sync with roughly half of the country, reflecting a serious national divide.

Washington High School is the hub, and the industries, the houses, and the business establishments radiate from that hub. Washington is an integral part of the Westside. The school has been around as long as most of the inhabitants.

It's not surprising to meet pupils at GWHS who have classes with teachers who taught older brothers and sisters - or mothers and fathers.

Figure 21 GWHS in the background, 1970s

Throughout the Vietnam conflict, the city of Indianapolis showed relatively mild enthusiasm for the kind of active protest against the war that had erupted in other cities. Even after events such as the My Lai massacre and the Kent State killings, the activism tended more towards candlelit prayer services than public marches and protests.[130]

Eddie Bopp, a student at Washington in the early sixties and a teacher/coach there during the seventies, reflected back on this period of change. "Unrest and disorder, which had infected our nation in the late 1960's [the Civil Rights and the anti-war movements] created tension at Washington High."[131] He felt strongly that the disruptive events of the late sixties and seventies had seriously damaged a positive sense of history and community that had always been taken for granted at Washington.

> Too many bits and pieces of the social network of the Washington community had vanished, most by the mid-1970s. The Mothers' Club, Businessmen's Club, Intramural Fund, class Athletes of the Year, fund raising events (specifically the Continental Capers), PTA, school plays and musicals, Homecoming floats and dances and even the in-school publishing of newspapers and yearbooks had vanished by the 1980's.[132]

While change during this period was difficult, the causes of this disruption can certainly be debated. Bopp's perspective on the consequences reflects one who grew up and spent his life in Hawthorne. He remembered a more stable time socially.

School Closings

In the 1950s and 60s, the traditional idea that public schools were created for the benefit of the immediate neighborhood residents was changing. Beginning in the 1960s, the Indianapolis Public Schools (IPS) was faced with a series of challenges to do with the shifting geography of social class, race, sources of school funding, and educational opportunity. White flight to the outer suburbs left remaining historic neighborhoods increasingly poor and under funded. The result was a weakening of support for the neighborhood school. Declining enrollments from 100,000 in the mid-1960s to 47,000 in 1992 resulted in school closings and reorganization to address these declining student numbers.

Enforcement of the 1973 federal court ruling that required busing to achieve desegregation in the IPS system further complicated the conflict between the city and surrounding suburban schools such as those on the Westside.[133] It wasn't the desegregation issue itself, however, that appeared to cause the strongest immediate reaction in Hawthorne, although that was certainly an important factor. It was the earlier Indianapolis Public Schools' (IPS) decision in 1970 to change the Hawthorne School (the historic IPS School #50) from a K-8 school to a K-6 school. This particular change to K-6 had immediate and serious consequences for families and for the neighborhood, and it is remembered as a significant turning point in Hawthorne's history. It meant that kids graduating from the sixth grade would now have to be bussed out of the neighborhood to the nearest middle school for two years before they would be able to return to the neighborhood to attend George Washington High School. They were bussed up to School #61 north of 30th Street in Speedway, leaving behind a community-based school with long traditions and support networks and going to an unfamiliar school without that kind of direct local support. Many of the parents were outraged at the change and threatened to leave the neighborhood if they were able.

> With that changing [to] K-6, it seemed like people started to move then. That's when I think people . . . they would stay here 'til their kids reached 6th grade, or close to that. But once it got to 7th and 8th well then their kids would have to be bussed to a Middle School or Junior High somewhere. Then they would move.[134]

Over the next few years in IPS, one school after another was closed, primarily because of low enrollments and budgetary problems. After the loss of local jobs, it was busing and school closings that had the most traumatic impact in Hawthorne. The school closings happened over a twenty-five year period beginning in the early 1970s. Although this seems like a long and gradual shift, every closing took a serious and irreversible toll on the community that surrounded it.

IPS School #16 just east of Hawthorne, a historic school built by the early Indianola community in the area that later came to be known as Stringtown, was the first to close, in 1973. Stringtown had been hit by a series of destructive events in the first half of the century leaving them vulnerable to forces of change: the devastating flood of the White River in 1913, the Depression that hit them particularly hard in the 1930s, and even more by World War II when some of its houses were destroyed to make room for expanding factories. It never completely recovered from the cumulative effects of those events. IPS School #30 (John McCormick School), another Stringtown historical landmark, closed in 1980. Then came the closing of the Westside's high school, George Washington High School, in 1995. Even Hawthorne's beloved School #50 (Nathaniel Hawthorne School), the historical center of the community with extremely close ties to the Hawthorne Center and the neighborhood, closed two years later in 1997.[135]

The impact of all these school closings was devastating to Westside neighborhoods. Community schools are a principal anchor for residents. They keep families invested in the neighborhood and provide multiple opportunities for people to connect with and support one another. They help to identify and train local leadership, to define the character of a community, and to provide it with a sense of permanence and predictability. As important institutions in the socialization of members of the community, schools are remembered forever by virtually all who grew up in a particular area. Reunions, homecomings, and fairs all symbolize the ongoing relationship between schools and members of the community, whether young or old.[136]

The closing of a neighborhood school immediately affects a much larger number of families than other types of change. Even if anticipated, it is a sudden impact that changes everything in the life of a community. The fact that similar changes were taking place throughout IPS did not lessen the anger or the shock of local residents who felt abandoned by the city and a loss of control over their children's future.

Churches Decline

The fifties was a period of prosperity for the churches in Hawthorne. The sixties was a transitional period, and the seventies and eighties a period of precipitous decline in membership. As families left the neighborhood and schools and businesses closed, the churches naturally suffered declining membership and attendance. By 1991, for example, only 58% of St. Anthony's members remained in the Hawthorne area code.[137] After moving away from the neighborhood some families returned for Sunday services for a while, but that loyalty did not last. In a neighborhood where community had been maintained by members who lived within walking distance of the church a decline in resident members contributed to a decline in the well-being and spirit of the community. The loss of community was deepened by the growing number of newcomers who did not claim membership in any of the local churches.[138] The oldest congregations in Hawthorne responded to the crisis with varying degrees of effort, but usually without success. The challenges facing them were overwhelming.

Washington Street United Methodist Church

Washington Street United Methodist Church membership, at one time topping 300, had dropped into the thirties by the late 1990s, with an average attendance of 25 at their weekly services. It became a major challenge to pay the pastor and church staff. Various adjustments were made in personnel and programs, and some support arrived from more prosper congregations in the city. But creative and devoted efforts could not halt the spiraling decline of membership.

Even with reduced resources, Washington Street UMC made genuine attempts to serve the needs of the neighborhood in the few ways that they could: a limited food pantry, and a program for teaching basic English to newly arriving Spanish-speaking peoples. A 1998 interview with the pastor gave a discouraging report.

> The number of renter-occupied housing units in Hawthorne is increasing. Some people rent rooms in houses and buildings converted into multi-unit housing. Absentee landlords control much of the tenant property. Care for income property is often

lacking. The neighborhood is in the midst of a transition from working class to poor.[139]

The church had failed to establish ties with the new population in the neighborhood, and there was a gradual breakdown of the community spirit that once existed. Even the part-time pastor was commuting to the church only three days a week from Bloomington, and usually returned home after the Sunday worship service.

By the 1990s 75% of their members lived outside the neighborhood, most commuting from their new homes much further west where they had moved in recent years for jobs, or better schools, or to escape the effects of a neighborhood in decline. As membership declined, the grip of history and fond memories and loyalty to the community was loosened, and the bonds finally ceased to hold.

A look at Washington Street UMC membership through the decade of the nineties provides a dramatic picture of precipitous decline in the community, a persistent theme in many urban neighborhoods at this time.[140] During this brief period the congregation changed, from a reduced but still functional membership that retained a vision of possibility, to finally closing their doors.

YEAR	MEMBERSHIP	AVERAGE ATTENDANCE
1992	134	39
1993	128	37
1994	121	31
1995	121	31
1996	112	25
1997	112	25
1998	54	23
1999	45	25
2000	43	25
2001	0	0

Figure 22 Washington Street UMC Membership and Attendance, 1992-2001

United Methodist Church Archives, DePauw University, Indiana

Washington Street Presbyterian Church

By 1996 the Washington Street Presbyterian Church, a much smaller church, was in a similar situation. The church considered its parish to include the three neighborhoods: Haughville, Stringtown, and Hawthorne. But after 1970 the congregation could no longer financially support a full time pastor. By 1996 over fifty percent of the church's budget came from outside sources. The parish was 60% Whites, 40% Blacks, and "a small but increasing number of Hispanics." But only about a third of the congregation actually lived in the parish.

A "Mission Study Report" indicated that membership was down from a peak of about 450 in 1936 to an average attendance of 43 in 1995. The report acknowledged that Michigan Street was "a strong racial boundary, separating blacks to the north and whites to the south," and that the reality of that boundary was reflected in the church's membership: "While we contend that our congregation is open to embracing people of other cultures, we still have many members who are very uncomfortable with the idea." The actual membership in 1995 was White, older, and predominantly female. It suffered from revolving pastoral leadership and a lack of real connection with the neighborhood, and was struggling to keep the doors open.[141]

West Park Christian Church

West Park Christian Church, the first Protestant church constructed in Hawthorne, was also unable to survive the neighborhood decline. Its official membership in 1998 was 101, but there were only ten or twelve regular attendants in the Sunday Worship Service. Most of the members were older. All were White, all from Hawthorne, and most were female. This church, once the most active and largest congregation in Hawthorne (See fig. 19.) now did not have the sources or income sufficient to fund real programing or outreach to the community.

The pastor's attempt to engage the congregation in even small programs of outreach to the newly arriving Mexican population was unsuccessful. As the neighborhood's Hispanic population increased significantly in the 1990s, there was some discussion about considering an Indianapolis Hispanic pastor's request to share their building for Spanish services, but ultimately they did not agree to it.[142] Like the other churches at this time, West Park Christian Church was barely surviving, a condition that did not mix well with their failure to reach out and embrace changes in the neighborhood.

St. Anthony's Catholic Church

St. Anthony's membership, mostly working class and poor and most over age fifty-five, was officially 1,240 in 1998, a number that bore little relationship to actual attendance figures. It drew from a large area, including beyond the immediate neighborhoods. Two hundred and fifty member families lived outside the parish, some quite distant; but less than a quarter of these members even attended Mass. Partly for that reason it had lost what was once a very strong sense of community, and members' active involvement in the church seemed limited to attendance at Mass.

Although St. Anthony's did not have a successful outreach effort, its official membership in the late nineties reflected a more ethnically diverse congregation than any of the protestant churches. There were three active African American families, and 136 Hispanic members. But the Hispanic members (Mexican) attended a separate Spanish Mass that they had initiated themselves. They had only recently requested and received permission to use the church building (See Ch.11). Largely because of the initiative of this growing influx of Mexicans, St. Anthony's membership suggested a viable though struggling congregation.[143]

* * *

By the late nineties, attending members in all of the neighborhood protestant churches consisted predominantly of older folk, many of whom resented the neighborhood changes taking place that they could neither accept nor escape. They lacked the funds and motivation necessary to overcome significant barriers. To some extent St. Anthony's was exceptional because recent Mexican arrivals had sought out the only nearby Catholic Church and formed a new Spanish-speaking congregation. The churches, once a vital thread in the fabric of a healthy homogenous community, were now among the last vestiges of that struggling community.

The Closing of George Washington High School (1995)

George Washington High School had been a focal point of Westside history since its opening in 1927. Its closing in 1995 was the proverbial last straw for an area whose multi-faceted struggle in recent years had been unrelenting. The impact of this closing was felt on all of the attending neighborhoods equally. The recounting of its closure offers an additional window on to the role of public institutions in keeping communities alive, and on the impact of shutting down a community school.

As IPS continued to deal with the economic consequences of its declining student numbers, Washington High School stood out as having the lowest enrollment (1,227 students) of the seven city high schools. As rumors of the possible closing began to spread, reactions came from every quarter. In 1994 the *Indianapolis Star's* Dick Cady interviewed a number of attendees at Washington High's 12th Annual Reunion (300 attended!) about the possibility of the school closing and summarized their feelings. "Closing Washington High School, as IPS may do," he wrote, "would be tantamount to grinding into the dirt an entire enclave of the city and the multicultural heritage it represents." Washington's former long-time Principal, Cloyd Julian, said: "We're not just talking about saving Washington High School. We're talking about saving the Westside."[144]

An outspoken pastor of Washington Street Presbyterian Church in Hawthorne, Rev. John Koppitch, represented the feelings of folk in this area when he made an impassioned appeal in the *Indianapolis Star* to keep the high school open, accusing the city of consistently dealing unfairly with its poorest areas.

> I serve a community devastated by the loss of six neighborhood schools. Areas around the empty, boarded-up and deteriorated school buildings are among the worst in the city. In our entire parish area (Haughville, Hawthorne, and Stringtown neighborhoods) only two public schools remain, School #50 [Hawthorne School] and Washington High School. That the most stable residential areas of our parish surround these two schools is no accident. Our neighborhood churches, resident organizations, community centers and development corporations will be hard pressed to overcome the destructive effects of yet another abandoned school building. Further, previous school closings, combined with the busing of our black children to township schools,

have effectively eliminated Near-Westside parents
from participating in the much-heralded Select
Schools program. And now our high school is to be
closed as well? To solve racial imbalance problems
in township schools, it is our children who are
bused all over the county. To solve IPS' financial
woes in the late 1970s, it was our neighborhood
elementary schools that were closed. To solve the
present financial crisis, it is our high school that
is on the chopping block. Why should families of
one community suffer the burdens of system-wide
problems not just once but over and over again.[145]

State Representative Paul Cantwell echoed this sentiment in a
brief comment: "This would mean one big hole in the Westside.
You might as well close the community." An IPS board member,
Donald Payton, bitterly attacked the closing: "They might as well put
a fence around the Westside and call it the Westside industrial park
or something."[146]

Despite local sentiment and demonstrations, the school finally
closed in 1995. School #50 (Hawthorne School), the last public
school in the Nearwestside, closed two years later! The Director
of the Hawthorne Center, Diane Arnold, who had grown up in
Hawthorne, attended Hawthorne School and graduated from
GWHS, recalled the closings and its immediate impact upon the
stability of the community.

They closed all of the schools. So literally we were
a community with no public schools whatsoever. All
of the children in our neighborhood were bussed out
to make the racial balance for other schools . . . We
lost lots and lots of people who had the resources to
move to Decatur or put their kids in Decatur Schools
or moved away into a Township. Lots of people. So it
was pretty traumatic.[147]

Arnold continued with a more specific description of the
consequences of that closing.

When the high school closed, high school aged kids in the neighborhood stopped going to school! They didn't make the *segue* to Northwest [Northwest High School] where they were now supposed to attend because that meant they had to get up and get on the bus stop at 6:30 in the morning. When Washington was open, if they didn't get up until 8:30 or 9 o'clock or 9:30 they could still walk to Washington and get the majority of their school day in. They just didn't make that. I would say the dropout rate in this community, in Stringtown and Hawthorne, went as high as 80%. Our kids just stopped going. So we lost people. People moved out if they had the resources to move out. They couldn't sell their houses so they started renting their houses, which meant that we had more transients; we had more people that weren't part of that stable fiber of the community. Drop out rate went higher; unemployment rate went higher. Factories had closed. So it really had a very negative impact on our community.[148]

* * *

From the 1960s to the late 1990s Hawthorne was forever changed by a number of devastating developments over which they had no control. The major plants closed. Then the factories connected with the rail lines closed. Local retail businesses struggled and then moved to the suburbs or went out of business. Longstanding residents began to leave. Many single-family properties became rentals.

The 1973 U. S. District Court order initiating school busing for desegregation further encouraged the exit of families with children. The schools closed—all of the grade schools and the only high school. Most of the churches, after years of trying to cope with change and declining membership, finally closed their doors. The Hawthorne neighborhood was left without the network of institutions that had anchored their community for decades.

Hawthorne had become a very different neighborhood.

CHAPTER 11

Living in a Changing Neighborhood: A New Beginning

The Hawthorne neighborhood's prosperity and well-being reached its height in the 1950s. At that time every sector of the neighborhood was flourishing. Churches, schools, and businesses each had their own important spheres of influence that overlapped with others contributing to a strong civic community. And all supported the Hawthorne Center in a variety of ways. After three decades of overwhelming disruption in the neighborhood, however, the Center was left practically alone among local institutions as it struggled to maintain and expand its programs to address the mounting needs of residents.

The Low Point

By the 1990s conditions in Hawthorne reflected years of decline. Physical deterioration in the neighborhood was a challenge. Crime, domestic violence, and drug abuse had increased significantly, and residents didn't feel as safe in their community as they once had. Police presence became a more common sight in the neighborhood. By this time children in Hawthorne, and in the Westside generally, were being bused to 14 different schools. Growing numbers of students were either skipping classes regularly or dropping out of school altogether. Church membership and attendance was in a steep dive.

Growing numbers of families moving out led to an increase in absentee landlords and declining house values. There was a palpable distrust of the city bureaucracy whose policies were blamed for much that had gone wrong over the years, most recently busing and school closings. Although Hawthorne was still predominantly a White working class neighborhood, there was more racial diversity now than in the past. By the mid-90s the breakdown was: 80% White, 10% Black, and 10% Hispanic, with Hispanic numbers increasing rapidly.

And yet, reflected the Director of the Hawthorne Center in a 1995 interview, there were still positives. Despite the common negative mantra "things are not like they used to be," a number of residents, both old and new, still expressed a commitment to the neighborhood. The neighborhood's regular activities such as street fairs, family nights at the Center, sports events, and holiday celebrations continued to be held. There still seemed to be some community spirit, though obviously much weaker now. A Black church (Second Baptist) had moved into the neighborhood, even though most of its members did not actually live there; and they were making efforts to participate in neighborhood activities. The Center's new board members were active and included representation from an increasingly diverse population.[149]

Just days after this optimistic interview, George Washington High School closed, followed two years later by the closing of the historic Hawthorne School (IPS School #50), the last public school in the area. These two closings were catastrophic for Hawthorne and for the Nearwestside, a final blow to a number of families with children at all educational levels who now would have to be bused out of the area to attend both elementary and secondary school, or else relocate to another area. This was the neighborhood's low point.

The Newest Immigrants: Hispanics

The arrival of Hispanics in Hawthorne coincided with the neighborhood's final slide towards its low point. As we have discussed, this was not the first wave of immigrants or newcomers to arrive in the Westside. In the late nineteenth century Eastern Europeans came as laborers in the new industries, settling predominantly in the Haughville area and bringing with them different languages and cultural behaviors that set them apart from the other neighborhoods emerging in the Nearwestside. Germans and Irish moved into the Stringtown area for the same reasons. They tended to define themselves, at least initially, as outsiders. After World War II, African-Americans largely from the south moved into neighboring Haughville, and migrants from southern Appalachia replaced the Germans and Irish living in Stringtown. Movement of newcomers into Nearwestside neighborhoods, introducing both ethnic and social change, had been a persistent theme in Westside history, as in Indianapolis.

The traditional Hawthorne neighborhood had always managed to remain relatively unaffected by the influences of these new residents that appeared mostly in surrounding neighborhoods, at least until the seventies and eighties when social and economic changes became more pronounced and challenged the relative stability and isolation that once characterized Hawthorne. It was the cumulative effects of the closings, the growing number of cheap rentals, lowered house prices, and vacancies that opened wide the doors of the Hawthorne neighborhood to outsiders. And this time it was Hispanics (predominantly Mexicans) who walked through those doors.

The arrival of Hispanic residents in the 1980s was a very visible change in the neighborhood, particularly as they began to open businesses in stores that had been vacated along Hawthorne's stretch of Washington Street. By this time the city of Indianapolis had already experienced a growing Hispanic population and had begun to recognize and support it.[150] Although the Hispanic presence in Indianapolis went back a few decades, their numbers had been very small, and there was limited public awareness of their presence. This changed in the sixties and seventies, first with an influx of Cuban refugees fleeing from the changes wrought by the 1959 Castro revolution, and then with an increase in internal migration primarily from California and from the northwest Indiana-Chicago region.

The 1970 U. S. Census indicated a Hispanic population in Marion County of approximately 6,700, though the real numbers were arguably much higher. St Mary's Catholic Church in the center of the city offered the first regular mass in Spanish beginning in 1967. In 1969, WFMS-FM radio began offering a one-hour program every week that featured Hispanic music and social events, as well as information about the city and work opportunities.

The 1970s and 1980s were decades of accelerated growth for the Hispanic community in Marion County, both in terms of population and organizations. The city's increased media coverage of the Hispanic community reflected that growth. Several Protestant denominations organized Spanish-speaking congregations. In 1971 local leaders founded El Centro Hispano (the Hispanic Center), with wide support from the Roman Catholic Archdiocese and the Church Federation of Greater Indianapolis, and from the mayor's office (Richard Lugar). It's purpose was to provide the growing Hispanic population with services such as locating housing, English classes, job counseling, help with naturalization, and other services that required translation.[151] The Greater Indianapolis Hispanic Chamber of Commerce was formed in 1984 to assist Hispanic-owned businesses. Several new activities and organizations appeared on the Indianapolis cultural scene.[152]

The pattern of Hispanic settlement in Indianapolis was quite different from other larger cities. In Indianapolis Hispanics did not settle only in one place that created a kind of *barrio,* as was the case in Chicago, for instance. Instead, individuals or families would simply find housing they could afford wherever it was available in the city and settle there, attracting friends or family to them when possible. The result was the emergence of small clusters of Hispanics appearing all over the city. Hawthorne's Hispanic population was one of those clusters.

A few people of Mexican heritage had already begun to settle in the Nearwestside in the 1980s. One of the first to settle in Hawthorne was Celia Parra. Her story is a common one at that time.[153] As the oldest child in her family, forced to provide for her family, at age 34 she left her four young children with her parents in Guadalajara, Mexico to look for work in the U. S. In 1977, with the help of a *coyote,* she traveled from Tijuana to Los Angeles in the back of a truck packed with about twenty other workers. From there she was flown to Chicago where, with no education and no English, she got her first job working in a Hilton Hotel kitchen and began to plan for bringing her children to the States. Chicago had developed a sizable and permanent Mexican population going back several decades creating a Spanish-speaking neighborhood that became a popular cultural haven for new arrivals in the mid-west.

When friends convinced Parra that opportunities were better in Indianapolis, she moved there in 1984. She found a house in Hawthorne and settled with her children and worked in the kitchen of a local downtown hotel for the next twenty years. In 1987 she and her children received temporary resident status under the federal Amnesty Immigration Act of 1986, a first step towards citizenship. Parra and her children were among an estimated 1,150 immigrants who applied for and received legalization in Indiana at this time.

Life in Indianapolis was difficult at first, Parra recalls. She usually walked the long distance to work downtown, or took local transportation when she could afford it. Because of her ethnicity she was not always accepted, and lack of English continued to be a problem. Nonetheless, she helped other members of her extended family come to Indianapolis, some of them settling in Hawthorne near her. She felt that the work and pay were very good and the housing cheap, especially compared with Chicago. She and her family were able to save and buy a house. Her daughter opened one of the first Hispanic businesses in Hawthorne, and was the first Mexican recruited to serve on the Board of the Hawthorne Community Center.

Parra also encouraged friends from Chicago to come to Indianapolis. She helped them find jobs and settle, and sometimes gave them loans to help purchase a house. As word spread, she became a major contact person in the area for other Mexicans who arrived, even when she did not know them. They would show up at her door asking for information on jobs or places to live. Some purchased houses as soon as they were settled and working regularly. Some rented apartments or houses in Hawthorne temporarily. It was the beginning of a small cluster of Hispanic families.

Despite transportation difficulties, Parra was not isolated from the Hispanic population scattered about the city. While working downtown she managed to visit the Hispanic Center located on North Street where she learned about their activities and networks. She occasionally volunteered there and was able to make friends and useful contacts. She also volunteered at the Hawthorne Community Center serving as a useful bridge between the Center and the small local Hispanic population. Although Hispanics living in the Nearwestside were represented in all three neighborhoods, the 2000 Census indicates that the actual Hispanic population in Hawthorne by that time (548) had increased to eighteen percent of the neighborhood's total population, double that of the other two neighborhoods. [154]

PRIMARY ORGANIZATION	TOTAL NEIGHBORHOOD POPULATION	NUMBER OF HISPANICS (mostly Mexian)	NO. OF VACANT DWELLING UNITS
Hawthorne Neighborhood Association	3025	548	189
Haughville Community Council	7187	234	625
Stringtown Neighborhood Association Council	1884	255	144

Figure 23 Nearwestside Hispanic Population and Available Housing

2000 U. S. Census, Block Level data

Vacant buildings along Washington Street were an attraction for some Hispanic entrepreneurs. They had arrived at a time when many businesses essential to a fully functional community had fled. With minimal investment, there was space for the more enterprising among them to experiment with opening a business. In an eight-block stretch of Washington Street (between Belmont and Warman Streets), the traditional "main street" for the Hawthorne neighborhood, no Hispanic businesses appear in the 1990 Census. But more than a dozen appeared in the 2000 Census in that same area indicating a decade of significant turnover. Hawthorne's main street changed during that ten-year period presenting a significantly altered façade and business environment. [155]

Figure 24 Former Site of Huddleston Restaurant

The response of the local Anglo community could have been to celebrate a rejuvenation of businesses along the Washington Street strip, but that didn't happen. For instance, the Huddleston Restaurant, a very popular family restaurant that had finally closed in the nineties, now became occupied by Taqueria La Frontera, another restaurant but with a very different menu, not exactly a replacement for the Huddleston Restaurant. Many of their customers were strangers to the neighborhood that didn't speak English. In the beginning non-Hispanic local residents were extremely reluctant, some of them fearful without reason, to patronize this and the other new businesses. It wasn't what they were used to, and some felt threatened by the differences. The Masonic

Lodge and Temple, a popular meeting place for Masons and their families, became a Hispanic night club (Phone Ana Express). The site of the Bonsett Press was occupied by *La Ola Latino Americana*, the first Spanish newspaper in Indianapolis. The appearance of a local newspaper had been long absent from Hawthorne. However, not only was *La Ola* published primarily in Spanish, there was no local news. Instead the paper targeted the Hispanic community scattered throughout the city.

1990 Property Status	2000 Property Status
became	
(vacant)	Botania El Milagro
(vacant)	Inter Call
(C & B Auto)	Gonzales Grocery Store
(Bull Winkles Used Furniture)	Aguascalientes Records
(Bonsett Press)	La Frontera
(")	La Ola Latino Americana
(Masonic Temple)	Phone Ana Express (night club)
(vacant)	Imagen Telecommunications
(Bunk House: mfg)	Princessa Beauty Salon
(apartments)	Maria's Travel Agency
(Huddleston's Restaurant)	Taqueria La Frontera
(Benny's Economy Bakery)	La Explosiva
(F S F Safeway, Personnel Dept.)	La Voz de Indiana

**Figure 25 Emergence of Hispanic Businesses
in Hawthorne in the 1990s**

Polk City Directories 1989 and 2001 of Marion County, Indiana

The closing of so many Anglo businesses reflected the end of a long struggle of Hawthorne's business community for survival. The new Hispanic businesses did not supply the majority Anglo population with what they were used to, but they filled some unsightly empty stores with activity and color and began a revival of Hawthorne's main street. It was a dramatic visual announcement of the presence of these new residents who now could meet some of their own basic needs using their own language and feel more at home. The outside world that passed through this strip of Washington Street at this time began to refer to it as "Little Mexico."

In Hawthorne, evidence of this growing Mexican population was also reflected in the churches. The majority of the Hispanics (not all) were Catholic. A small group of Mexicans, led by Celia Parra, approached the priest at St. Anthony's, the only Catholic Church in Hawthorne, requesting space so that they could organize a Spanish mass. She recalled that meeting.

> We talked to him and he did the Celebration. It started with four people. We gave out flyers. . . Once we got started, we began to fill the place. . . After some time they saw that the place was too small for us. So they gave us permission to do the ceremonies in their San Antonio church. Now we fit.[156]

This was a significant service to the local Mexican population. By the 1990s Protestant churches in the area were also being approached with requests to use their now available space for holding Spanish language services.

The struggling Washington Street UMC, a much older working class congregation, received outside funding to support a moderately successful Survival English School for Hispanic arrivals. But the pastor was mostly on his own in reaching out to the new arrivals—trying to learn Spanish, attending gatherings of Hispanic clergy, and looking for bilingual leadership that could help attract Hispanics. Despite the genuine efforts of the pastor, however, the small struggling congregation was not very supportive. The church ultimately closed down, and the building was soon after occupied by Vida Nueva, a United Methodist Hispanic congregation with a Hispanic pastor who had moved his congregation from the Eastside of the city and now thrived in this new location.

Figure 26 La Vida Nueva UMC (formerly Washington Street UMC)

Figure 27 La Vida Nueva UMC (Announcements)

Further east the Washington Street Presbyterian Church was in a similar predicament, making its final attempts to reach out to

Stringtown and Haughville as well as Hawthorne for new members, including Protestant Hispanics, but with limited success. It shut down and was later occupied by a Protestant Hispanic congregation. The struggling West Park Christian Church congregation also resisted reaching out to Hispanics.

The Hispanic population, a small minority, was now increasingly visible in the neighborhood. Their new businesses were a reminder of change. Their kids were bused to schools along with the rest of the community's children and shared classrooms with their Anglo neighbors. They began to participate in the Center's sports programs and to connect with the Center in other ways, especially through the child daycare program. Both adults and youngsters organized their own soccer teams that played at the nearby Hawthorne Park or the vacant grassy fields belonging to the Central State Hospital west of the neighborhood. They were, in fact, bringing some revitalization to Hawthorne.

Many of the Hispanic residents sought relief from the pressures of living in a different culture through participation in their recently established Spanish-speaking congregations every Sunday, but their day-to-day interactions with the host culture were sometimes challenging. The Hawthorne Center led the way in modeling an attitude of acceptance and in seeking ways to integrate its newest residents. In 2004 the Director of the Center offered an upbeat comment on the changed neighborhood.

> I love living in a diverse community. There are times that I feel a little overwhelmed. Certainly when you drive down Washington Street it's almost like being in another country. I kind of like that. I think if you live in San Francisco, you pay big money to live in a diverse community. I think we're pretty fortunate that we have it here. There's much to do and to learn from each other.[157]

Support from the City

By the early 1960s some in the city of Indianapolis had begun to wake up to the need for urban development. The focus of government at this time was on the downtown, so they did not prioritize peripheral neighborhood problems until much later. However, there were folk sympathetic with the goals and work of the longstanding Settlement Movement and its related organizations, and also familiar with the work of community centers in Indianapolis. In 1959 they met to consider ways of helping struggling neighborhoods. They organized the non-profit Indianapolis Settlements, Inc. (ISI) to evaluate the extent of the problems in the neighborhoods and to develop a structure and a plan through which they could help communities address their problems. They determined that the best approach would be to work through the existing neighborhood community centers.

> It was recognized that no one agency can provide all the services needed by a neighborhood. Yet the settlement [community center] may serve as the catalyst which brings other agencies into the area to provide needed programs and the settlement also can provide the communicating link between all the agencies serving the neighborhood.[158]

ISI's earliest efforts focused on four identified "Operating Divisions" (community centers) on the Westside, also sometimes referred to as "settlements": Christamore House (Haughville), Hawthorne Center, Concord Center (Near-Southside), and Southwest Social Centre. Stringtown, having no equivalent organization through which to work, was not directly represented, but ISI encouraged Hawthorne to extend their work there. ISI Executive Director, Mrs. Alfred Dobrof, began to hold meetings with these community centers and encouraged them to cooperate with each other in dealing with their problems. She pressed each to survey their neighborhood with the goal of developing long range plans for dealing with the growing problems.

The work progressed slowly. Historical differences between neighborhoods, as well as ISI's internal organization and funding challenges, slowed the efforts. Ultimately, however, each of the neighborhood centers succeeded in conducting its own survey and producing a report of conditions in their neighborhood, with recommendations for improvement. In 1968, ISI combined these early surveys from four neighborhoods they had worked with on the Westside that had community centers. Then they wrote a covering summary of the findings and attached it to the neighborhood reports. This combined report became a baseline study of conditions in this area and set the tone for ISI's work in other parts of the city.[159]

This study was useful for shaping the ongoing work of the centers, particularly for highlighting "the responsibility of Settlement Boards [the community center boards] to take action on issues which effect the lives of the neighbors." In other words, the neighborhood community centers were now seen as the primary local leadership for addressing neighborhood development and well-being. Given the social and economic challenges of this new era, it was an awesome responsibility that in earlier years had belonged to a host of now absent local business leaders and community groups. ISI did a good job of helping the centers begin to identify their problems and plan for how to deal with them, and it facilitated recruitment of some local sources of funding. But this good work did not result in any significant funding resources from the city until the 1990s, twenty-five years later.

Hawthorne had always been responsible for recruiting its own human and financial resources, which during the good years were drawn heavily from within the neighborhood. More recently those resources of necessity had come from outside the neighborhood, including a number of religious organizations, and charitable organizations such as United Way of Central Indiana. In 1983, in an attempt to bring order to the increasingly competitive and confusing funding process for community centers, and to equitably distribute available funds, these various funding organizations came together and created the Community Centers of Indianapolis (CCI), "a federation of multiservice centers" that now provided a single source of funding to the centers.[160] This was helpful for centers that were having a problem acquiring and managing funding, but much less so for the centers that had already become reasonably successful in raising and managing their own funds, such as Hawthorne Center.

The initial ISI report makes it clear that Hawthorne had fewer problems than the other neighborhoods and had already developed it's planning and programs to address many of the recommendations suggested by the report. Regarding the need for the community centers' boards to do more to include the participation of neighborhood residents in the making of policy and program planning, for instance, the ISI report remarked:

> One center, of course, Hawthorne, has always had a neighborhood Board. The others are recognizing more and more the importance of involving neighborhood residents in the decision making process .

And

> The Hawthorne neighbors, who have *justifiably* [our italics] prided themselves that they have maintained a stable, solid, law abiding neighborhood in the face of many threats.

Although Hawthorne Center was perhaps better prepared than nearby neighborhoods, it was still suffering from neighborhood decline, and Center leaders felt that the work of ISI was helpful in preparing it for the coming challenges.

In 1982 the Indianapolis Department of Metropolitan Development (DMD), in collaboration with existing neighborhood organizations, conducted its own survey and plan for improvements, but it failed to target or prioritize the specific areas of greatest need. And it produced few concrete results. According to DMD's later admission, Federal, State, and Local funds directed at the neighborhoods in the years following that study were not "sufficient to address all of the housing problems which have existed in deteriorating neighborhoods . . . Public investments made sporadically throughout the Near Westside neighborhood have not, in most cases, induced noticeable improvements on surrounding properties."[161]

In 1994, in response to growing recognition of neighborhood problems, the DMD once again conducted a study of the three Nearwestside neighborhoods to determine needs and develop a plan for improvements. The 1994 DMD report, "Nearwestside Housing Improvement and Neighborhood Plan," was the main product of that effort.[162] Having learned from its past mistakes, it now aimed to target four of the most needy areas in each neighborhood, assist each neighborhood in producing a 5-year block level strategy for dealing with these areas, and prioritize each component of the neighborhood's plan, thus enabling the Centers to know exactly where to channel whatever government and non-government funds entered the area. Increased funding from the city made possible this much more thorough effort, and it brought some stability and permanence to the city's on-going commitment to its neighborhoods.

The Changing Role of Hawthorne Center

With the declining fortunes of the area since the 1960s, Hawthorne's dependence on outside funding had increased. With it came pressure on the Center to extend its responsibilities beyond traditional boundaries. Haughville had its own community center (Christamore House) and programs to meet neighborhood needs. But Stringtown, the neighborhood to the east, did not have a center. It had struggled for years to establish a permanent local organization and leadership that could mobilize the community and consistently represent them with one voice, but this did not happen. When its residents needed social services, or wished to participate in team sports and other community activities, they were encouraged to use the Hawthorne Center. This was not a satisfactory solution, but the only one available.

To the west, the newer Southwest Multi-Service Center (serving the very large area of Mars Hill and Speedway) was in such serious financial straits by the 1990s that it was no longer able to serve its changing population. Responding to a request from the Community

Centers of Indianapolis (CCI), the organization that at that time controlled the flow of city funds to the neighborhoods, Hawthorne agreed to a merger with Southwest Multi-Service Center and extend some of its services to the west.

Although this was a temporary arrangement, it caused debate in Hawthorne over the limits of the neighborhood's responsibilities. It also raised a serious question about the problem of accounting and equitable distribution of the city's funds. Sometimes Hawthorne received extra funding for its extended responsibilities; other times it did not. Defining responsibilities and catchment areas for the service centers, and determining how to report the numbers served, became a troubling challenge. It further raised the sensitive question about the integrity of traditional neighborhood boundaries. Hawthorne's Center Director offered a small illustration of the problem of how to define and limit service to people within its traditional boundaries.

> We have people whose children go to the [local] Catholic school [All Saints] who don't live in this neighborhood, but we provide childcare. So why would we not want to provide them with utility assistance and holiday assistance? People are more mobile now. Maybe [traditional] catchment areas are obsolete now? Strict boundaries don't make a lot of sense sometimes.[163]

In practice it had little choice. Hawthorne's role had changed as it expanded its services from an exclusive focus on the traditional neighborhood to a larger and less well- defined "catchment area" and to increased cooperation with its neighbors. By the 1980s and 1990s the wide range of local institutions that had once defined and anchored Hawthorne community were gone, or in their death throes. The neighborhood was now filled with a more diverse population, commonly strangers to one another, and poorer. Within the neighborhood, only the Hawthorne Center had the structure and leadership that could provide or channel the needed social services, as well as provide the physical and social activities that offered residents a chance to interact. In effect, the Center had become the primary voice of the neighborhood (and beyond), the go-to place for residents seeking social or economic help, and for resolution of other problems and conflicts. With help and encouragement from the city, and from other external sources of help, the Center expanded its programs and staff to meet that new challenge.

At this time the Center's leadership and core staff had grown up in the neighborhood and participated in Center activities for many years. They remembered what a vital civil society felt like and how it functioned, and what the Center's role in that supportive network had been. They understood that change had made it impossible to return to anything resembling those earlier days, but they worried over how to reconstruct a meaningful and responsive community in this new situation.

The Center's regular services at this time, many of them offered to folk beyond their neighborhood, included a wide range of programs: half-day pre-school programs for 3-5 year olds; a highly structured before-and-after-school youth program for 5-12 year olds; youth team sports activities; job assessment counseling, job referrals and follow-up; a program for Seniors age 60 and over that included shopping, educational programs, field trips, games, and a hot lunch; an emergency food pantry; some limited assistance for special needs; and a wide-range of responses to unpredictable social and economic needs. They spent substantial time pursuing financial support just managing the paperwork required by their funders, and participating in collaborative efforts to solve problems common to the larger Westside area. When time allowed they also tried to focus on the future: preventive measures for addressing the deeper causes of the problems, attempting to be "a fence at the top of the hill, not the ambulance at the bottom" the Center's Director was fond of saying.

The Center's youth programs had always appealed to the neighborhood kids, regardless of their family background or situation; and the adults were often pulled into contact with the Center through their children's participation in these programs. But the challenge was much more difficult now with the different economic circumstances and ethnic diversity of the residents. It could no longer take for granted a homogeneous population or the same level of local support.

The Anglos, even if they were recent arrivals and had no deep roots in the neighborhood, were at least culturally more familiar with how community centers functioned and their purpose. And they had no language barriers to participation in Center programs. The bridge to the recent Hispanic arrivals, however, was more difficult and evolved more gradually. In the beginning Hispanic families were very few and were accepted more easily by the existing population. In addition, their numbers were insufficient to develop their own support community, so they were more amenable to integration. Center Director Arnold recalls:

> Probably as early as ten or fifteen years ago [early 80s] we had a few [Hispanic] families. And those families were just part of the fiber of the community. They came to our neighborhood organizations. They supported whatever we did. Their children came to Hawthorne [Center].[164]

In the nineties Hispanic numbers in the neighborhood began to increase significantly.

> My first thought was these were relatives of people who were already here. [The numbers] kept growing. And then I kind of thought, you know, we really need to start looking at that. I just kind of noticed it but didn't really think much about what impact that had on what we did. Kept growing and growing and finally [I] said, we have to do something.[165]

Arnold and her staff realized that childcare was potentially the best way to connect with Hispanic families, especially for families where all the able-bodied adults worked outside the home, now a common practice. So the Center focused on providing them daycare, a challenge but ultimately successful.

So we literally had mothers bring their children in to us and putting their children in our staff's arms. The children were crying and hysterical. The parents were upset. My staff was upset, but nobody could even talk to anybody. We couldn't find out what was wrong with the child if the child cried during the day because the child didn't speak English.

The need was obvious. They needed someone who could help in working with those who only spoke Spanish.

The Center had always preferred hiring from the neighborhood whenever possible, so Director Arnold thought immediately of the Hispanic family that a few years earlier had moved into a house near to her parents a short distance from the Center. Arnold's account of what happened in that situation is a story worth presenting in full, for it shows clearly one of the positive ways in which the two populations developed initial relationships. First steps.

My father, who is from Kentucky, is probably not the most socially tolerant person in the world. We started noticing that [Hispanic] families were moving in. And two families moved in, two Spanish-speaking families moved in next door to my father. One was right next door . . . And so, I thought, oh this is going to be tough. My father is in his seventies. He doesn't hear well. He is going to have somebody next door to him that he can't understand. And my father is very gregarious and outgoing, so he is in the middle of whatever. Well, that first summer my father, he and my mother put twelve tomato plants out . . . So he would put [the tomatoes] in a bag and he would go next door and knock on the door, and they would come to the door and he would shove this bag of tomatoes toward them. Now, they couldn't talk with each other, but they'd smile. And my dad would smile. And so that went on for the whole summer. Well, in the fall, like in September, there was a knock on my parents' door. They opened the door and here's these little children, there's four children in their family, and they shoved a bag of apples. They'd gone to the apple orchard, and they shoved a bag of apples at my dad and mother. Well, in November my mother and father bought them, bought the family, a turkey assuming we had Thanksgiving so [they must] have Thanksgiving. So they gave them this turkey. Well, they prepared the Turkey with the green mole sauce and sent part of that Turkey back for them. And now it's this love fest!

Thereafter Arnold referred to her father as "my poster child for cultural diversity!"

One day she was talking to her father about why the Center needed to hire someone from the neighborhood that could speak Spanish and work with the children. "Five minutes later he brings the husband and wife over from next door . . . He'd gone over and gotten [the couple]. He'd brought [them] over to his house, and he said, 'I told [them] you wanted to hire somebody!'"

This family had come from Mexico, first to Chicago like so many Mexicans, and then on to Indianapolis pursuing a better opportunity. They had lived in the neighborhood for about four years, and at the time this story happened had recently bought a house. The father had a full time job, and the mother had already demonstrated responsibility and a strong work ethic at some jobs in the neighborhood. Although she was just beginning to learn English Arnold thought she would be a good investment and hired her to help bridge the cultural gap at the Center. She became the first Hispanic employee at the Hawthorne Center, "one of the Center's most valuable investments," says Arnold.

As the number of Hispanics grew in the nineties, so did social tensions. In some parts of the neighborhood, eager landlords saw the dramatic influx of Hispanics as opportunity. They bought up a number of single-family dwellings, divided each into five or six apartments, and rented them out for an affordable price. Neighbors might wake up suddenly to six families next door, six times as many cars, six times as many kids, and six times as much noise and trash! The landlords prospered. The neighbors panicked and grew angry. "They weren't angry at the landlord who was getting $3,000 a month for every house," exclaimed Arnold. "They were angry at the people who lived in the house!"

Stories circulated quickly in this small neighborhood, sometimes ramping up sensitivities and encouraging disturbing and often false rumors. There were, however, enough verified stories about Hispanic newcomers to excite popular concern, such as: "Strange men" were seen walking about the neighborhood. (True) Seven or eight men were seen going in and out of the cellar doors of a vacant house. (True) A long-time resident woke up to find a strange car parked in front of her house. (True) Representatives from the Westside Community Development Corporation (WESCO) went to check out a boarded up HUD house they were going to buy and prepare for new occupants, and they found several Hispanic males already living in it! As it turned out, someone was charging them rent illegally to live there! (True) The number of misunderstandings and potential conflicts increased, often owing to language misunderstanding.

> Literally a woman who could be born in her house in this neighborhood, could wake up one day and not be able to talk to her neighbors on either side of her. That overwhelming sense . . . that if they are talking a language I don't know they must be talking about me!

One incident was particularly upsetting to the Center leadership. Some kind of argument (unclear exactly what) began on a street corner between Anglos and some Spanish-speaking individuals. Anglos from the neighborhood were congregating. None of them could speak Spanish, and the Mexicans were short on English, so the situation escalated. Police were called in, but they couldn't understand Spanish either. A few days later at a neighborhood meeting in the Center residents discussed this incident. The Center Director was present and recalls what happened.

> And then people started with, "Well if THOSE people come, they need to learn our language." And "THOSE people are bringing drugs into our neighborhood." Well, I've lived here for forty-five years, and drugs were here before THOSE people got here! (laughing) I got real embarrassed; and this lovely [Mexican] family who had supported our community and been wonderful citizens got up and walked out of this meeting.

This incident was a primary catalyst for the Center's thinking about how to develop programs that might serve both ethnic groups. Most Center programs up to this point had been designed to target the whole neighborhood, as if residents were all the same. But the neighborhood was becoming increasingly diverse in many ways, socio-economically as well as culturally. You couldn't just design a program for one group separately.

In this new context it seemed that the challenges of language and culture were going to be the defining weakness of any neighborhood-wide program. So the Center staff began to consider programs that would address that issue, stepping carefully into the process "because if it appears we are over serving one population, or serving them at the expense of the other population, then we get in trouble."

Because of the Hawthorne Center's need to deal with a multicultural and sometimes disadvantaged population, and because of their work with the city on such problems, they were one of two neighborhoods in Indianapolis selected by the Annie E. Casey Foundation in the late 1990s to pilot a program called "Making Connections." In this program, a diverse selection (age and ethnicity) of 8-12 residents met in four "study circles" to confront and discuss local issues.[166]

The first thing they did was to directly confront the language issue by establishing a permanent ESL (English as a Second Language) program for local Hispanics, and a Spanish class for the neighborhood's Anglos, meeting at the same time! Their first effort was a two-hour program once a week for eight weeks. The last fifteen minutes of each class they put the two groups together, face-to-face with one another, and made them practice.

One exercise for those trying to learn Spanish provided the opportunity for the Anglos to visit the new Hispanic businesses on Washington Street. Afterwards they took them to eat at one of the restaurants where they could hear and practice simple Spanish. This particular activity struck at best a very mild blow against the cultural wall that had developed in the neighborhood against Hispanic businesses along Washington Street. The ESL classes, on the other hand, had discussions about very real problems: the city's transportation system, the role of the police (a big source of fear and misunderstanding among Hispanics), and other prominent neighborhood issues.

> In the beginning, it was tough. People weren't making eye contact. And people weren't comfortable. By the end of the eight weeks they had a pitch-in. And it was so funny because we brought meatloaf, and mashed potatoes, and macaroni and cheese; and they brought the quesadillas and the tamales wrapped in the corn shucks and the stuffing . . . And that's kind of what we've hit on, what things we can do in a community.

This model program was so successful that it was repeated a number of times in Hawthorne, and the model spread to other neighborhoods. It was the Hawthorne Center's participation in this program that emphasized their need to deal more preemptively with the issue of language and culture. The Center wrote its first proposal to Indianapolis' Community Development Block Grant program to fund a Hispanic outreach person, a Spanish speaker with clear instructions to focus on working with both Hispanics and Anglos. It was accepted.

Adding to the Center's challenges, drugs and crime had also increased in the 1990s in Hawthorne, as it had in many neighborhoods in Indianapolis and around the country. Residents didn't feel safe. And trust, so essential for a successful community, was in short supply. Police presence in the neighborhood had necessarily become more frequent. Many Anglos in the community blamed this increase on the growing number of Hispanics. Clearly such problems had appeared long before the Hispanics arrived, but the newest immigrants were most visible and made easy scapegoats.

Hispanic families, too, were fearful. Complaints related to security issues came to the Center from Hispanic families. For example, Hispanic businessmen complained about the police failure to protect their businesses from break-ins claiming discrimination against them because they were Hispanic. So the Center stepped in and hosted a meeting with some of the business folk, the Deputy Chief of Police, and other concerned citizens to discuss the problem and possible solutions. This kind of bridge building became a frequent part of the Center's program.

One of the concrete outcomes of this first meeting, in addition to helping break down barriers and stereotypes, was the organizing of Neighborhood Crime Watch groups to help police the area. At first, lack of familiarity with such efforts and lacking trust in the police, they had difficulty recruiting Hispanics to be Crime Watch leaders, or even to come to the regular meetings at the Center. By early 2000, however, that had changed.

> Of the fifteen [Crime Watch] block captains we have in this neighborhood, probably ten of them are Spanish-speaking. They come, and they are religious about coming to our neighborhood meetings. So we feel like we have made great headway with that.

The Crime Watch block meetings themselves became opportunities to respond to a range of residents' complaints and fears. In this way the Center has continued to play the role of honest broker in facilitating good relations between the community and the local police.

Sometimes incidents in the neighborhood were "learning moments" for the Center's leadership. For example, an issue emerged when a Hispanic nightclub on Washington Street (The Millennium) was applying for a liquor license. It was discussed at a neighborhood meeting, and there was near violent opposition to their being granted a license.

And I thought it was going to be Hispanic versus non-Hispanics, that the non-Hispanics would say we don't want this Hispanic nightclub. Well, to my amazement that's not the way it came down at all . . . It was the Mexicans that did not want the Dominicans! So it was interesting for me because this meeting almost got violent . . . That was the first 'hello' to me that, you know, there's not just Hispanic and non-Hispanic. There's Hispanic to Hispanic, based on other issues.

The recognition that not all Spanish speakers are the same and that they can differ on issues was an eye-opener for residents. Although most of Hawthorne's Hispanics were Mexican, they too were a diverse group. There were representatives of at least four other Hispanic nationalities living in the neighborhood. Not surprisingly, Hispanics also had the similar experience of generalizing about all Anglos.

There continued to be issues between (broadly speaking) the two major cultural groups. Since the language barrier was key, the Center began printing all information bulletins and newsletters in Spanish as well as English. But beyond language deeper problems confronted Hispanics and Anglos equally: unemployment or underemployment, drugs, safety, education, and poverty. The way that the Hawthorne Center dealt with these issues, without drawing attention to ethnicity, helped to build trust with both populations.

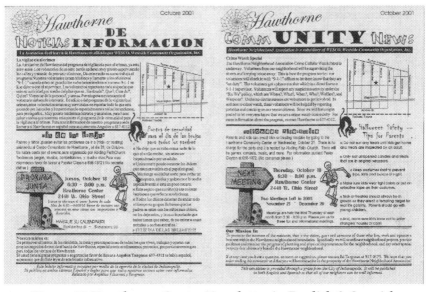

Figure 28 Hawthorne Center Newsletter in English & Spanish

The 1990s to the early 2000s had been among the most difficult years for the Hawthorne neighborhood as it struggled to recover economic and social stability and maintain some sense of community. The Center's deeply rooted local leadership and commitment to service insured that it would play a primary role in these efforts. They increased their budget and expanded their services. By the turn of the century, the Center's program had expanded into a range of programs and services managed by over thirty personnel, a level of community service that would have made the Center's founders very proud.[167]

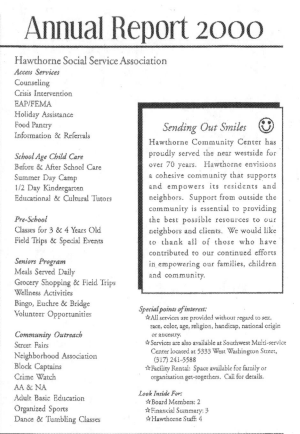

HAWTHORNE COMMUNITY CENTER

Annual Report 2000

Hawthorne Social Service Association

Access Services
Counseling
Crisis Intervention
EAP/FEMA
Holiday Assistance
Food Pantry
Information & Referrals

School Age Child Care
Before & After School Care
Summer Day Camp
1/2 Day Kindergarten
Educational & Cultural Tutors

Pre-School
Classes for 3 & 4 Years Old
Field Trips & Special Events

Seniors Program
Meals Served Daily
Grocery Shopping & Field Trips
Wellness Activities
Bingo, Euchre & Bridge
Volunteer Opportunities

Community Outreach
Street Fairs
Neighborhood Association
Block Captains
Crime Watch
AA & NA
Adult Basic Education
Organized Sports
Dance & Tumbling Classes

Sending Out Smiles ☺

Hawthorne Community Center has proudly served the near westside for over 70 years. Hawthorne envisions a cohesive community that supports and empowers its residents and neighbors. Support from outside the community is essential to providing the best possible resources to our neighbors and clients. We would like to thank all of those who have contributed to our continued efforts in empowering our families, children and community.

Special points of interest:
☆ All services are provided without regard to sex, race, color, age, religion, handicap, national origin or ancestry.
☆ Services are also available at Southwest Multi-service Center located at 5333 West Washington Street, (317) 241-5588
☆ Facility Rental: Space available for family or organization get-togethers. Call for details.

Look Inside For:
☆ Board Members: 2
☆ Financial Summary: 3
☆ Hawthorne Staff: 4

2440 W. OHIO STREET, INDIANAPOLIS, INDIANA 46222 (317) 637-4312

Figure 29 Hawthorne Center Annual Report for 2000

One of the principal reasons for the Center's success was the continuity and personal commitment of the Center's leadership, a common reality in other community centers. During Hawthorne's most significant period of change, from the 1970s to the early 2000s, the Center was fortunate to have just two Directors guiding their programs, virtually a family tag team: Marie Kenley (mother) and Diane Arnold (daughter).

Marie and her husband grew up in eastern Kentucky. Her husband was a mechanic with McLean Trucking Company. When McLean moved to Indianapolis in 1958 the family moved with them and settled in the Hawthorne neighborhood just a few houses from the Center. Marie's first contact with the Center began when she volunteered with the Girl Scouts who were meeting there. She expanded her volunteer work with the Center in several areas until the current Director recognized her abilities and offered her a part-time job and a free hand to develop some new programs. Among other things she started a popular daycare program that became a permanent part of the Center's offerings. Her success led to a full time job and growing administrative responsibilities in the Center's work. In 1973 she was hired as Director of the Center. It was a perfect fit. The Board all agreed she had demonstrated the skills and the personal commitment to understand and manage the challenges confronting the Center during a time of tremendous change. She held this position until her retirement in 1986.[168]

Her daughter, Diane (Kenley) Arnold, was five when she arrived in Hawthorne with her family. She grew up in their house just down the street from the Center. The Center and its programs was literally her world as a child. She hung out in the Hawthorne Center where her mom was working. She went to the nearby Hawthorne School #50 and spent much of her after school and free time participating in Center activities. When Arnold was 15 she began working at the Center as a dance teacher, and continued to do various jobs there over the years as she attended grade school and Washington High School. She went on to IUPUI (Indiana University Purdue University Indianapolis) in Elementary Education graduating in 1975, and a few years later returned to get her Masters Degree in Social Work and Management, a combination that fit perfectly with her Center experience and with the Center's needs.

Diane never really lost touch with the neighborhood or the Center. After teaching for a year at a local parochial school she returned to the Hawthorne Center to take charge of Social Development programs. When her mother stepped down from the position of Director, despite her mother's warnings about the heavy responsibility and the work hours Diane decided to apply for that position. The Board elected her to head the Center in 1986 creating a smooth transition of leadership and continuing her mother's commitment and work.[169] She helped to steer the neighborhood through some of its most difficult years and held this position until her retirement in 2018.

Figure 30 Marie Kenley Passing Keys of Hawthorne Community Center to Daughter, 1986

The founders of the Hawthorne Center decades earlier could never have imagined that the center would someday come to completely dominate response to the neighborhood's social and economic needs. In the beginning the Center was only one among a number institutions that formed the neighborhood's civic infrastructure, what its founders would have considered an ideal situation. In the last three decades of the century, however, those institutions had gradually disappeared from the neighborhood leaving the Hawthorne Center mostly alone to provide a range of vital services and activities in difficult times, and serve as a the primary connector between the neighborhood and external agencies.

Rebuilding

Five years after its closing, in the fall of 2000, George Washington High School reopened as George Washington Middle School offering 6th, 7th, and 8th grades for over 600 students.[170] During those intervening five years much had happened in the Nearwestside that was primarily responsible for the re-opening. When clamorous protests had failed to prevent GWHS's closing, local efforts formed the Westside Education Task Force in 1998 that committed to the hard work of mobilizing the neighborhoods and pressing city officials to reopen Washington, and to provide "a school that serves families and neighborhoods as well as students."[171]

Figure 31 Front Cover of Community News, July 26, 2000

This group formed a diverse partnership of public sector and community organizations, businesses, and family and community groups, including: Westside Cooperative Organization (WESCO); West Indianapolis Neighborhood Congress; Hawthorne Community Center; Christamore House; Mary Rigg Neighborhood Center; Indianapolis Public Schools; IUPUI; Lilly Technologies; Indy Parks; Indianapolis Metropolitan Police Department; National Starch; the Annie E. Casey Foundation; and some local community and business partners. Its success was facilitated by the IPS shift away from the 1970s federal court order for cross-district busing back to a more "community schools" model. The opening of Washington Middle School showed what was possible: "When a school and a community truly work together to connect kids and families to economic opportunities, social networks and effective support, both succeed because both are strengthened."[172]

By the 1990s conditions in the neighborhoods and the schools had become familiar to all: an increase of violence (including domestic) and drug abuse, increasing discipline problems and violence in schools, increased absenteeism in the schools, increasing absentee landlords in the neighborhoods accompanied by declining house maintenance and property values, and a host of other consequences of social and economic instability. All of these problems encouraged the Task Force to take more seriously the idea that the education of students must be seen in a broader community context, and to understand that a successful school must offer more than a traditional curriculum to effectively address these conditions.

In pursuit of this aim the new GWMS aimed to provide an ambitious range of services: English Language classes (for non-English speakers) and Spanish (for the dominant non-Spanish speakers); EvenStart GED and preschool programs; school-based child health care and family counseling services (staffed full time); a full-day kindergarten (in partnership with Hawthorne Community Center); year-round recreational opportunities (in partnership with Indy Parks); and a program of conflict resolution skills for students (staffed by two full-time counselors).[173]

The new school was housed in the old GWHS building located just inside the Hawthorne neighborhood. Since the Hawthorne

Community Center had been so closely involved in the life of George Washington High School since its founding it was now able to play a major role helping the Task Force to understand the local situation and conditions, and to construct the new Middle School programs. For the Hawthorne Center, the restoration of the school was deeply personal. Residents and kids and grandkids would no longer have to take the bus to a distant school. They realized that the damage done to Hawthorne and surrounding neighborhoods by all of the closings could not be undone; but the return of a genuine community school to the area promised the possibility of rebuilding anew, perhaps with a school that could address the new circumstances more effectively than had the old school.

The opening of George Washington Middle School received national attention for its holistic approach to community education and was seen as a model for future IPS schools. The neighborhoods represented on the Task Force renewed their efforts to cooperate in building links between families and the school, and they continued to push George Washington towards full high school status. Their experience of working together in the Task Force had forged new connections and relationships that would, they believed, represent the neighborhoods and their different populations, and support a more unified approach to future endeavors. The Hawthorne Community Center, representing the Hawthorne neighborhood, was as always on the frontline in confronting these challenges. As the new century began, although change and challenges continued in the neighborhoods, it seemed a hopeful time.

CHAPTER 12

What's in a Name?: Recounting the Story

There have always been important threads of shared experience between Hawthorne and its neighbors to the east and north, Stringtown and Haughville. To mention a few: news from the locally published *West Side Messenger* during the early years; decades of academic and sports activities of George Washington High School; decades of coping with the challenges of a declining area that disrupted the neighborhoods' populations and changed the direction of their historical narratives. Yet these three neighborhoods also have very distinct histories, and they always recognized and acknowledged their differences.

It is worth recalling several ways in which the Hawthorne neighborhood differed from the other neighborhoods. Historically the farmland that later became Hawthorne was considered part of Haughville's 1883 incorporation. Yet it developed physically separate from Haughville, initially without a clear name or identity. Hawthorne emerged considerably later than the other neighborhoods in a context of ethnic and class homogeneity, a White "100% American" residential population settling in a small area of open farmland (the Warman farm). Hawthorne's boundaries were fixed and limited from the start and changed little: the railroad tracks south of Washington Street formed the southern boundary. Haughville, north of a different set of railroad tracks, and Stringtown east of Belmont Avenue, completed Hawthorne's enclosure. The extensive grounds of the State Asylum for the Insane (Central State Hospital) prevented expansion westward. Industrial development and most employment opportunities lay just beyond its boundaries making it a totally residential community.

The Hawthorne Community Center, an important actor in Nearwestside development, was built by and for the neighborhood residents in the years after World War I largely through affordable memberships and small local donations, which did much to strengthen the community's identity. "It's OUR Center!" was spoken frequently and with pride.

By the 1990s the story of Hawthorne's once thriving civil society had changed profoundly. During those years of decline Hawthorne gradually surrendered its image as a vibrant successful neighborhood. "Newcomers" had replaced many of its original residents, but they were unable to rebuild the economic and social infrastructure that had once sustained it as a prosperous neighborhood and community. Nor could these new residents identify with the stories of events and personalities from the neighborhood's past. For both outsiders and newer residents, then, "Hawthorne" was becoming a name without an associated sense of its history.

There is another reason for the public's lack of knowledge about Hawthorne's history. Initially George Washington High School's founding and early leadership grew out of the meetings of the Hawthorne Association in the early 1920s. Washington's continued connections with Hawthorne's feeder School #50 and the Hawthorne Community Center were strong, and were an important part of Hawthorne's history. As GWHS grew and drew in students from all of the Westside neighborhoods, however, its growing popularity created a broader more inclusive story that gradually and quite naturally overshadowed individual neighborhood issues and histories.

An unfortunate misnaming that accompanied the city's growing involvement in the Westside's development at this time also reduced the public's awareness of Hawthorne as an independent historic neighborhood. In the process of seeking more collaborative and convenient ways to assess problems and allocate resources for development during the city's belated focus on neighborhoods, representatives from the city and some non-profits began to treat the three distinct neighborhoods (Hawthorne, Stringtown, and Haughville) as a single unit, evidenced by their frequent reference to the "Nearwestside," without clarification. Along the way the word "neighborhood" was increasingly attached to that name. For instance, in 1982 the city's Department of Metropolitan Development (DMD) published the "Nearwestside Subarea Plan" and described it as "an overall neighborhood plan." The "subarea" was the three independent neighborhoods. Use of this newly designated umbrella term began to spread. In 1994, as part of Mayor Goldsmith's focus upon development in the city's neighborhoods, once again the DMD published the important "Nearwestside Housing Improvement and Neighborhood Plan." In this report the term "Nearwestside" was more clearly elevated to neighborhood status, and the three historically distinct neighborhoods were consigned to sub-neighborhoods. (See fig. 32.)[174]

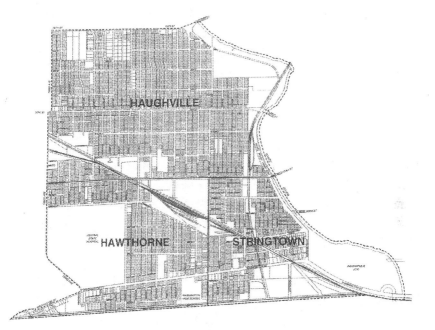

MAP 3
SUB-NEIGHBORHOODS

NEARWESTSIDE NEIGHBORHOOD

April 20, 1994

The preparation of this map
was financed in part by a
Community Development Block Grant

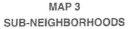
N

Department of Metropolitan Development
Planning Division   *Imagis*
Indianapolis - Marion County, Indiana

**Figure 32 Three Historic Neighborhoods
Reconfigured As Sub-Neighborhoods, 1994**

This might seem an insignificant action. However, as this
designation began to be used more commonly it was treated as if it
was a single neighborhood, increasingly assuming a level of unity
and commonality that did not actually exist. When researchers

and developers in the 1990s began to construct a brief history of the city's Westside, they tended to conflate narratives of the three historic neighborhoods into one "Nearwestside Neighborhood." The term became, quite naturally, a name in search of its own historical narrative. And it found one.

In the early 2000s when the Polis Center at IUPUI (Indiana University and Purdue University at Indianapolis) produced its online "Study Neighborhoods" as part of its larger city-wide "Project on Religion and Culture," it provided a single historical narrative for the three neighborhoods, and of course used (inaccurately) the name of "Near-Westside Neighborhood."[175] This project had carried out an impressive work of collecting narrative histories and timelines of nineteen "historic neighborhoods" in Indianapolis in the late nineties. Yet, risking repetition here, the Near-Westside is *not a historic neighborhood* in any meaningful sense of the word. It is an area composed of three distinct historic neighborhoods that share boundaries and a few major challenges and historical developments. To be fair, this online Polis historical narrative begins by clearly acknowledging that the "Near Westside Neighborhood" is actually composed of the three different historic neighborhoods. But it then proceeds to combine a very uneven selection of events from the three distinct neighborhood histories into a single narrative, at best confusing to the reader, at worst suffering important omissions and distortions of balance and context. This was particularly true for Hawthorne neighborhood.

Gathering the three neighborhood histories under a broad umbrella term into one account with a new name is understandable in some circumstances. For instance, it is useful for the convenience of certain development projects that otherwise would have to deal with three separate plans. Similarly it was useful, even necessary, for George Washington High School to project this broader kind of perspective in order to not favor one neighborhood over another. Even in this short work we have had to use the term frequently as we drew upon sources that used it. But there is a cost to this. When you force multiple individual histories into a single narrative you risk losing the local perspective and the historical details that give importance and meaning to specific events and people's actions. You deny the residents of each neighborhood their own story, which is important for building a sense of belonging and commitment. And you deprive the public of an accurate historical account.

Of the three historic neighborhoods in this area, the Hawthorne neighborhood suffered most from this conflation, despite its historical importance. It was the newer neighborhood, and the smallest, so perhaps more easily overlooked in the broader search for history on the Westside of the city. Nonetheless, it is the only one of the three historic neighborhoods whose history was not listed in the massive Index of the celebrated 1994 *Encyclopedia of Indianapolis*, the public's go to source for historical information about the city. Nor was it listed as a neighborhood under that book's Subject Guide to "Places and Localities." Nor did it appear in the larger section on "Overview: Neighborhoods and Communities?"[176] Hawthorne Community Center, the long-standing institution known to all, earned one brief sentence in a discussion of community centers.

The term "Nearwestside Neighborhood" had become so commonly used by the 1980s and 1990s that references to that part of the city were less likely to be able to name actual historic neighborhoods. Names of prominent places should be valued as carriers of important stories, particularly if they have bestowed such benefits to the city as Hawthorne has done.

The city's long and detailed interaction with Hawthorne as a separate entity clearly gives it de facto status as a historic neighborhood. Why there is no account of it in the first thorough and inclusive history of Indianapolis is a puzzle that invites further research. Such omissions have negative consequences. This book is an attempt to recover a story that should in future be attached to its accurate name, the "historic Hawthorne neighborhood."

Endnotes

1   David J. Bodenhamer and Robert G. Barrows, eds. *Encyclopedia of Indianapolis* (*EI*) (Bloomington, IN: Indiana University Press, 1994).

2   Edward A. Leary, *Indianapolis: A Pictorial History* (Virginia Beach, Va.: The Donning Company, 1980), 34.

3   Ibid.

4   A. Hurtado, S. A. Roberson, and Jan Shipps, "Stringtown Survey Report," *Indiana Historical Sites & Structures Inventory* (Indianapolis: Center for American Studies, 1985), 5-7.

5   *Indianapolis Star*, "Mt. Jackson, City's First Suburb, Will Relive Era at Reunion Today," June 23, 1940.

6   Samuel W. Durant, "Plan of Indianapolis" [map], in *Maps of Indiana Counties*, 1876, reprinted from *Illustrated Historical Atlas of the State of Indiana* (Chicago: Baskin, Forster & Company, 1876).

7   *Indianapolis Star*, "Mt. Jackson, City's First Suburb," 1940.

8   This first schoolhouse was said to be located at 3232 West Washington Street, but it is clearly marked on Bohn's 1889 map of Indianapolis (See fig. 3) in a different location, between National Road and Jackson Street. Early records back to 1801 during the period of early frontier settlement in the area make reference to "the red brick schoolhouse". Gustav Bohn, "Mt. Jackson" [map], scale: 20 rods per inch, in *Atlas of Indianapolis and Marion County*, Revised from county records, surveys, and plat books of Hervey B. Fatout (Philadelphia, PA: Griffing, Gordon and Company, 1889)

9   Ollie Baus, "History of Mt. Jackson Cemetery" (paper presented at the meeting of the Wayne Township Historical Society,

Indianapolis, IN, May 1, 1967).

[10] Jerrold Footlick, "Stringtown? Neighborhood with a Past But No Name," *Indianapolis Times*, April 15, 1962. Stringtown refers to the wedge-shaped area just west of the White River, extending west to Belmont Street, between Michigan and Washington (See fig. 1). In recent years it has lost some of its eastern residential area to the development of the Indianapolis Zoo.

[11] Jacob Piatt Dunn, *History of Greater Indianapolis*, vol. 2 (Chicago: Lewis Publishing Company, 1910), 440; Durant, "Plan of Indianapolis" [map]; Cathleen F. Donnelly, "Kingan and Company," *EI*, 870-71.

[12] Hester Anne Hale, *Indianapolis: the First Century* (Indianapolis: Marion County-Indianapolis Historical Society, 1987), 86 and 103; Donnelly, "Stringtown," *EI*, 1306; Donnelly, "Kingan and Company," *EI*, 870-71; Deborah Markisohn, "Link-Belt Company," *EI*, 919; Footlick, "Stringtown?."

[13] Leary, *Indianapolis*, 45-80.

[14] James J. Divita, *Rejoice and Remember, 1891-1991* (Indianapolis: St. Anthony Parish Centennial Committee, 1992), 4-5.

[15] Gerry LaFollette, "Mt. Jackson: Center of City's Growth to the West," *Indianapolis Times*, January 21, 1962.

[16] Washington Street United Methodist Church, *Golden Anniversary of the Washington Street United Methodist Church, 1924-1974*, souvenir program compiled by the church (Indianapolis: 9 June 1974).

[17] Jacob Piatt Dunn, *Indiana and Indianans: A History of Aboriginal and Territorial Indiana and the Century of Statehood, vol.2* (Chicago: The American Historical Society, 1919), 440-41.

[18] Ibid.

[19] LaFollette, "Mt. Jackson."

[20] Dunn, *Indiana and Indianans*, 441.

[21] Divita, *Rejoice and Remember*, 7.

[22] Ibid.; St. Anthony Church, *St. Anthony Church*, a history of the church compiled for their Diamond Jubilee Celebration (South Hackensack, N. J.: Custombook, 1966).

[23] Divita, *Rejoice and Remember*, 15. These original Platt Maps and

Covenants are located in the Indiana Marion County Recorders Office archives.

24 Wayne Township, Marion County: Interim Report, *Indiana historical sites and structures inventory* (Indianapolis: Historic Landmarks Foundation of Indiana, 1993). The majority of the houses in this area today were built during the first decade of the 20th century. A survey done in this area in the 1980s of the historical sites and structures north of Washington Street (then referred to as "Haughville Historic District") provides estimates of the dates of home construction for all streets. Approximate dates, east to west: Belmont, 1900 and 1910; Sheffield, 1900 and 1910; Pershing, 1930; Tremont, 1920 and 1930; Mount Street, 1910 and 1920. Most of the houses west of Mount Street were dated 1910, with a few dating back into the 1890s and early 1900s.

25 West Park Christian Church, *West Park Christian Church 50 Year History*, a booklet compiled by the Jubilee Committee of the Church (Indianapolis, 1955).

26 Nathaniel Hawthorne School, "History of School 50," typescript compiled by the staff of Nathaniel Hawthorne School, 75 North Belleview Place, Indianapolis, Indiana, 1953. Growing enrollments led to the addition in 1911 and 1914 of eight new rooms to the school, including indoor toilet facilities. By 1953 there were lavatories, a medical room, an auditorium seating 225, a principal's office, cafeteria, and a teachers' room. In 1963 a new south wing was added to the building for the Junior High, and the junior high division of School #30 started going to Hawthorne School.

27 "West Park Christian Church 50 Year History."

28 "Golden Anniversary of the Washington Street United Methodist Church, 1924-1974." See Fig. 26 for a current picture of the church.

29 Lawrence J. Downey, *A Live Thing in the Whole Town: The History of the Indianapolis-Marion County Public Library, 1873-1990* (Indianapolis: Guild Press of Indiana, 1991), 151.

30 Ibid.

31 Leary, *Indianapolis*, 79; Monte Hulse, "Overview:

Neighborhoods and Communities," *EI*, 135.

32   Divita, *Rejoice and Remember*, 29-30.

33   Ibid. Divita. What follows is a summary of Divita's rather lengthy account of the conflict, important here as an illustration of early formative differences between the neighborhoods of a forming Hawthorne and Haughville.

34   Ibid., 30 and 82.

35   Footlick, "Stringtown?"; Cynthyia Clendenon, "Flooding and Flood Control," *EI*, 582.

36   Divita, *Rejoice and Remember*, 43-44.

37   Mark E. Schneider, "World War I," *EI*, 1460-62.

38   German Chancellor Otto von Bismarck was long dead, but was nonetheless held responsible for Germany's rise to power, a major cause of World War I. U. S. Army General John J. Pershing commanded the American Expeditionary force that was sent to fight the Germans in Europe.

39   "Hawthorne Community House Commemorates 25th Year With Mortgage Burning," *West Side Messenger*, January 6, 1949. The earliest copy of the *West Side Messenger* that could be found, a 1927 publication, came from George Washington High School's private collections (See Fig. 10.) The Indiana State Library has a few scattered holdings from later years.

40   A lengthy account of these beginnings appeared in an article highlighting an interview with Baker: "West Side Messenger Founded 52 Years Ago By Rev. C. G. Baker," *West Side Messenger*, November 15, 1967.

41   *West Side Messenger*, November 11, 1927.

42   See the sub-section below, "Not All Rosy."

43   "The New Deal Challenge to Marion County Democracy," *West Side Messenger*, June 7, 1934.

44   Harold Baker (son of Rev. C. G. Baker), telephone interview with author, June 16, 2004; "West Side Messenger Founded 52 Years Ago."
Rev. Baker sold the paper in 1934 to Toney Flack from Speedway. Flack set up an office at 2927 West Washington Street. (*West Side Messenger*, August 21, 1936). He owned and edited the paper until after World War II, and also began to

charge a small amount for the paper (5 cents per week, or $2 per year) in 1943 during World War II. Both news and advertisements then begin to reflect a gradual movement away from the central focus on the Hawthorne/Mt. Jackson area.

45 For several years the public used the name "West Park" to describe the growing residential area. Some considered it to be part of Mt. Jackson. By the 1920s, however, West Park had begun to overshadow Mt. Jackson. At the same time the name of "Hawthorne" was becoming more common and beginning to replace the name of both "West Park" and Mt. Jackson. The outcome of this shift is discussed in the final section of this chapter, "Naming the Neighborhood."

46 There are a number of local accounts and newspaper articles that describe the story of the founding of Hawthorne House, and they mostly agree on the main story, differing only in minor details. See, for examples: "West Park Social Service House, Costing $20,000, To Be Dedicated Formally Sunday," *Indianapolis News*, February 27, 1924; "All Work and No Play May Make Jack and Jill Dull Children and All Play and No Work May Make Them Ne'er-Do-Wells So Community Folk Try Remedy," *Indianapolis News*, July 12, 1930; "Hawthorne House Enters Twelfth Year of Service," *West Side Messenger*, January 11, 1935; Jerrold K. Footlick, "Hawthorne: Homey Area on West Side," *Indianapolis Times*, June 17, 1962; "Hawthorne Social Service Association, 50th Anniversary, 1923 to 1973," a program produced by the Hawthorne Association for their anniversary celebration [1973].

47 Excerpt from the Constitution of the Hawthorne Social Service Association, Article II, cited in the Association's program to celebrate the "50th Anniversary, 1923-1973," located in the Hawthorne Center collection.

48 Selected sources for the founding of Hawthorne Center are listed in footnote 46.

49 "Pastor Resigns in Controversy with the Klan," *Indianapolis Times*, July 31, 1923. See a discussion of the Klan's activity in Hawthorne below in section "Not All Rosy."

50 Footlick, "Hawthorne: Homey Area on West Side."

51 "Hawthorne House Enters Twelfth Year of Service," *West Side Messenger*, January 11, 1935.

52 This rendering of the three structures belonging to the Hawthorne Association appears on the cover of a booklet produced by the Hawthorne Social Service Association in 1973 to celebrate their "50th anniversary, 1923 to 1973."

53 "Hawthorne Community House Commemorates 25th Year."

54 "The Hawthorne Social Service Association," *West Side Messenger*, November 2, 1934.

55 Ibid.

56 *Indianapolis News*, "All Work and No Play," 1930.

57 Ibid.

58 Diane Arnold, interview by author, Indianapolis, January 21, 2004.

59 Information about the founding and early years of GWHS was gathered from several sources: early copies of *The Surveyor* (the school newspaper); the *West Side Messenger*; the George Washington High School Historical Collections; city newspapers; and from Hazel Corwin's "A Brief Summary from the Historical Record of George Washington High School, 2215 W. Washington Street, Indianapolis, Indiana, 1927-1985" (paper presented to the Wayne Township Historical Society, Indianapolis, 1985). Corwin was a 1936 graduate of George Washington High School.

60 "Washington High School Pupils Trained in Social and Civic Duties As Well As in Academic Studies," *Indianapolis News*, March 15, 1929.

61 A detailed summary of Rev. Baker's long talk was printed on the front page of the *West Side Messenger*, November 9, 1934.

62 Harold Baker, telephone conversations with author, May 22 and June16, 2004. Harold Baker, the son of Rev. C. G. Baker, grew up in Hawthorne and attended GWHS.

63 Cloyd Julian, interview by author, Indianapolis, IN, April 23, 2004; Cloyd Julian, *My Story*, (Greenfield, Indiana: Mitchell-Fleming Printing, 2002); "Washington High's 50th Year," *Indianapolis News*, May 24, 1977.

64 Dick Cady, "Older Grads see Washington as an Anchor for the

Westside," *Indianapolis Star*, May 5, 1994.

65   James J. Divita, "Demography and Ethnicity," *EI*, 56.

66   Jannette Covert Nolan, *Hoosier City: The Story of Indianapolis* (New York: Julian Messner, 1943), 282.

67   LaFollette, "Mt. Jackson."

68   These advertisements appeared in the *West Side Messenger*, Nov. 11, 1927.

69   LaFollette, "Mt. Jackson."

70   *West Side Messenger*, November 9, 1934. Eddie Bopp has included a brief history of the Workingman's Friend in his book, *Indianapolis Washington High School and the West Side*, 181-83. This local bar/restaurant has remained well-known and popular up to the present.

71   "Golden Anniversary of the Washington Street United Methodist Church: 1924 – 1974."

72   "Winners of City High School Championship," *Indianapolis News*, January 21, 1937.

73   Robert Howard, "Forum: The Readers Corner," *Indianapolis Star Magazine*, September 19, 1962.

74   The Polis Center, "Near Westside: Narrative History" (Indianapolis: The Polis Center, 2018).

75   Divita, *Rejoice and Remember*, 82.

76   Betty Harris, interview by author, February 25, 2004; H. Baker, telephone conversations, May 22 and June 16, 2004;.

77   Leonard J. Moore, *Citizen Klansmen, the Ku Klux Klan in Indiana*, 1921-1928 (Chapel Hill: University of North Carolina Press, 1991), 7.

78   Ibid., 146-9, 238.

79   *Fiery Cross*, vol.3, no.8, Indianapolis, Marion County, 21 December 1923, p.9.

80   "Hoosier Profile," *Indianapolis Times*, August 3, 1946.

81   Edwin L. Becker, "1923: Year of Peril for Indianapolis Disciples Pastors," *Encounter* (Autumn 1993), 375-76.

82   "Pastor Resigns in Controversy with the Klan," *Indianapolis Times*, July 31, 1923.

83   "West Side Messenger Founded 52 Years Ago By Rev. C. G. Baker;" Baker, telephone conversation, June 16, 2004.

84 Washington Street United Methodist Church, "Golden Anniversary," 18-20.

85 Divita, *Rejoice and Remember*, 76.

86 The Polis Center, "Near Westside: Narrative History."

87 Corwin, "A Brief Summary."

88 Julian interview, 2004.

89 Divita, *Rejoice and Remember*, 31-44.

90 *Indianapolis News*, "All Work and No Play."

91 Footlick, "Hawthorne."

92 Crumrin, "World War II," *EI*, 1463-5.

93 Corwin, "A Brief Summary from the Historical Record of George Washington High School."

94 Crumrin, "World War II," *EI*, 1465.

95 *West Side Messenger*, "Hawthorne Community House Commemorates 25th Year."

96 Ibid.

97 Jan Shipps, "Religion," *EI*, 180.

98 "West Park Christian Church 50 Year History."

99 Divita, *Rejoice and Remember*, 79.

100 Julian interview, 2004.

101 Ibid.

102 *West Side Messenger*, "Hawthorne Community House Commemorates 25th Year."

103 Hawthorne Social Service Association, "Program Report," typescript manuscript, prepared by the Program Committee of the Association, 1966.

104 Downey, *A Live Thing*

105 "Parents Protest Library Closing," *Indianapolis Times*, September 1, 1955.

106 Open Letter to the Hawthorne Teen Service Club, in "Hawthorne Happenings" [1960], a newsletter distributed to club members by the Hawthorne Community Center; Marie Kenley, interview by author, March 26, 2004.

107 Divita, *Rejoice and Remember*, 98-9.

108 Minutes of the Hawthorne Social Service Association Board Meeting, 21 December 1959; Mrs. Alfred Dobrof, Report Submitted to the Hawthorne Social Service Association Board

of Directors, 25 April 1960.

[109] Mrs. Alfred Dobrof, typescript of "Address Given at the Annual Meeting of Hawthorne Social Service House Board of Directors," at West Washington Street United Methodist Church, 23 May 1960.

[110] Minutes of the Hawthorne Social Service Association Board Meeting, 10 September 1962.

[111] Hawthorne Social Service Association Program Report, 1966-1967, 1 June 1966.

[112] "Working Paper for Hawthorne Self Study," typescript, 25 November 1968. Some of those registrants may have come from the poorer "Stringtown" neighborhood to the east of Hawthorne since Hawthorne Center, under ISI recommendations, now included it in their service catchment area.

[113] Arnold interview, 2004.

[114] Ibid.

[115] Ibid.

[116] "Neighbors battle on as last bank closes," *Indianapolis Star*, February 4, 1989.

[117] LaFollette, "Mt. Jackson."

[118] Hawthorne Community Center, "Report on Services and Programs," Indianapolis, September 1, 1965–March 1, 1966.

[119] Harris interview, 2004.

[120] Hawthorne Community Center, "Working paper for Hawthorne Self Study," November 25, 1968. This self-study was initiated and supported by Indianapolis Settlements, Inc.(ISI).

[121] "A Self Study to Determine Long Range Goals for Indianapolis Settlements, Inc.," Indianapolis Settlements, Inc. (ISI), (201 North Belleview Place, Indianapolis 46222), June 1969. ISI began in Indianapolis in 1959 and incorporated in 1965 as a non-profit agency for planning and coordinating services in the Westside neighborhoods. Under the direction of Executive Director Dorothy F. Unger, ISI produced this brief typescript manuscript, the first compilation of information from the Westside neighborhood community centers' self-studies of conditions in their neighborhoods (Christamore House,

Concord Center, Southwest Social Centre, and Hawthorne Social Service Center).

[122] For a detailed personal account of GWHS sports during these years see Eddie Bopp, *Indianapolis Washington High School and the West Side* (Bloomington, IN: Author House, 2010). Bopp grew up in Mt. Jackson ("Jacktown"), graduated from Hawthorne's School 50 and Washington High School. He played on Washington's basketball team in the 1960s during its most winning years, and later became a teacher/coach at GWHS. Bopp's book is a personal accounting, mostly of sports and sports personalities at Washington, but also includes a collection of short local biographies and stories from life in Hawthorne and his Mt. Jackson.

[123] R. Dale Ogden, "Basketball," *EI*, 307; William Dalton, "Football," *EI*, 589. Fig. 22 comes from the *Indianapolis Times*, March 21, 1965.

[124] *Indianapolis Star*, Front Page, March 21, 1965.

[125] Steve Hanlon, "Remembering Indiana's Titans," *Indianapolis Star*, November 24, 2000.

[126] Ibid.

[127] Ibid.

[128] Harris interview, 2004; Bopp, *Indianapolis Washington High School*, 159-60.

[129] Bopp, *Indianapolis Washington High School*, 19.

[130] Connie J. Zeigler and Thomas Keiser, "Vietnam War," *EI*, 1383-85.

[131] Ibid., 19.

[132] Ibid., 269.

[133] Michelle Hale, "School Desegregation Case (U.S. v. Board of School Commissioners)," *EI*, 1222-23.

[134] Harris interview, 2004.

[135] Marc E. Holma, "Reading, Writing, and Relinquish: The Abandonment of Historic Indianapolis Schools, 1970 to 1979," Master of Science Thesis, Ball State University, Muncie, Indiana, May 1998; Glory June Greiff, "Public Schools and the Neighborhood Life-Cycle," Historic Landmarks Foundation of Indiana, 1985.

[136] Tim Maher, "Schools and the Neighborhoods," in Greif, Glory-June, *Public Schools and the Neighborhood Life-Cycle, 1985.*

[137] Divita, *Rejoice and Remember,* 107.

[138] James J. Divita, in his review of Etan Diamond's *Souls of the City: Religion and the Search for Community in Postwar America* (Bloomington: Indiana University Press, 2003), raises the issue of the link between large numbers of unchurched individuals in a community and the search for community itself. (Indianapolis: H-Net, October, 2003.)

[139] Washington Street United Methodist Church, Main Census Final Report, from an interview by the Polis Center (IUPUI), Indianapolis, Indiana, September 16, 1998.

[140] Washington Street UMC, "Local Church Statistical Profile, 1992-2001," Indianapolis, Indiana. This report on "Membership and Worship Attendance" is housed in the Archives of Indiana United Methodism located in the collections of DePauw University, Greencastle, Indiana.

[141] Jim Dougans (pastor), "Washington Street Presbyterian Church Mission Study Report," typescript, July 12, 1996.

[142] Pastor John Neece, West Park Christian Church, interview by The Polis Center (IUPUI), Indianapolis, Indiana, September 16, 1998.

[143] Father John Ryan, St. Anthony's Catholic Church, interview by The Polis Center, IUPUI, Indianapolis, Indiana, September 15, 1998.

[144] Dick Cady, "Older Grads see Washington as an Anchor for the Westside," *Indianapolis Star,* May 5, 1994.

[145] "Impact of Closings," *Indianapolis Star,* May 1, 1994.

[146] Phillip Wilson, "Residents Try to Save Washington High," *Indianapolis News,* March 24, 1994.

[147] Arnold interview, 2004.

[148] Ibid.

[149] Diane Arnold, interview by The Polis Center, Indianapolis, Indiana, August 10, 1995.

[150] Although the Hispanic population in Indiana has diverse national origins, by far the largest number of Hispanics arriving in Indianapolis during this period were from Mexico. For a

brief history of Hispanics in Indianapolis up to the early 1990s see Charles Guthrie, Dan Briere, and Mary Moore, *Indianapolis Hispanic Community* (Indianapolis: University of Indianapolis Press, 1995).

151 Ibid., 16.

152 Briere, Guthrie, and Moore, "Hispanics," *EI*, 684.

153 Celia Para, interview by author [trans. by Dan Briere], April 28, 2004; "Amnesty Ends Immigrants' Lives of Secrecy and Fear," *Indianapolis Star,* May 15, 1988.

154 Information gathered from the 2000 Census Block Level Data.

155 Information taken from *Polk's Indianapolis city directory* (Marion County, Ind.), 1989-90, p.436 and *Polk city directory* (Marion County, Ind.), 2001, v.2, p.873.

156 Parra interview, 2004.

157 Arnold interview, 2004.

158 Dorothy Unger, Executive Director, Indianapolis Settlements, Inc., "A Self Study to Determine Long Range Goals for Indianapolis Settlements, Inc.," typescript monograph, Indianapolis Settlements, Inc., June 1969.

159 Unger, "A Self Study to Determine Long Range Goals."

160 Rosemary Dorsa, "Community Centers," *in Encyclopedia of Indianapolis,* 466-67.

161 Department of Metropolitan Development (DMD), "Nearwestside Housing Improvement and Neighborhood Plan," City of Indianapolis, DMD Planning Division, 1994, pp. 1-2.

162 Ibid.

163 Arnold interview, 2004.

164 Arnold, interview by The Polis Center, 1995.

165 Arnold interview, 2004. Unless otherwise indicated, the remainder of this section, including the quotations, draws primarily upon this interview.

166 The Annie E. Casey Foundation, an organization that works on behalf of disadvantaged children and families, provided funding for a "Making Connections" initiative in three cities: Des Moines, Indianapolis, and Seattle. Using their Study Circles model, they proposed to engage residents of a neighborhood in discussion and exchange activities that would strengthen

both families and neighborhood. The Hawthorne Center was one of two locations chosen in Indianapolis. For information on how this program works see: http://www.aecf.org/resources/family-circles-sharing-our-experiences/

167   Hawthorne Community Center, "Annual Report 2000." See Figure 28.

168   Kenley interview, 2004.

169   Arnold interview, 2004.

170   "Washington High School Reopens as a Middle School," *Community News*, July 26, 2000.

171   Don Payton and Diane Arnold, "Community United with Middle School," *Indianapolis Star*, September 26, 2000.

172   Payton and Arnold, "Community United"; Jim Grim, "Encouraging Better Schools by Drawing on Community Resources," *Indianapolis Star*, July 7, 2002.

173   Payton and Arnold, "Community United."

174   "Nearwestside Subarea Plan," Department of Metropolitan Development, Planning Division, Indianapolis, Indiana, 1982; "Nearwestside Housing Improvement and Neighborhood Plan," Department of Metropolitan Development, Planning Division, Indianapolis-Marion County, Indiana, April 20, 1994.

175   The "Near Westside" is one of the selected neighborhoods included in an on-line project created by The Polis Center entitled *Study Neighborhoods* (accessed July 23, 2019): https:\\polis.iupui.edu/about/community-culture/project-on-religion-culture/study-neighborhoods/?neighborhood=near-westside.

176   Bodenhamer and Barrows, eds. *Encyclopedia of Indianapolis*, 1994. There were three passing references to Mt. Jackson. The Hawthorne Center was merely named without description in the section on "Community Centers."

Primary Sources

Newspapers

Indianapolis Star
Indianapolis News
Indianapolis Times
West Side Messenger

Interviews

Diane Arnold, interview with Guthrie, Hawthorne Center, Indianapolis, 21 January 2004.

Harold Baker, telephone interviews with Guthrie, South Yarmouth, Massachusetts, 22 May 2004 and 16 June 2004.

Betty Harris, interview with Guthrie, Hawthorne Center, Indianapolis, 25 February 2004.

Cloyd Julian, interview with Guthrie, at his home in Indianapolis, 23 April 2004.

Margaret Marie Kenley, interview with Guthrie, in Hawthorne neighborhood, Indianapolis, 26 March 2004.

Celia Para, interview with Guthrie [trans. By Dan Briere], Hawthorne neighborhood, Indianapolis, 28 April 2004.

Carlos Ruiz, interview with Guthrie, Hawthorne neighborhood, Indianapolis, 22 February 2004.

Church Reports and Publications

West Park Christian Church
Washington Street United Methodist Church
Washington Street Presbyterian Church
St. Andrew's Catholic Church

Archives

Indiana State Library (Indianapolis), Newspapers and Clippings Files
Hawthorne Community Center Collection
Depauw University Methodist Archives
Indiana Historical Society (Map and Photo Collection)
Project on Religion and Urban Culture Archival Files, The Polis Center, Indiana University Purdue University Indianapolis
George Washington High School Historical Collection

City Directories

Polk's Indianapolis City Directory (Marion County, Ind.), 1989.

Polk City Directory (Marion County, Ind.), 2001, v.2.

U. S. Census Data

2000 Census Block Level Data, Indiana State Library, Indianapolis, IN.

Secondary Sources

Becker, Edwin L. "1923: Year of Peril for Indianapolis Disciples Pastors." *Encounter* (Autumn 1993), 369-80.

Bodenhamer, David J. and Robert G. Barrows, eds. *Encyclopedia of Indianapolis*. Bloomington, IN: Indiana University Press, 1994.

Bohn, Gustav. "Mt. Jackson"[map], in *Atlas of Indianapolis and Marion County*. Revised from county records, surveys, and plat books of Hervey B. Fatout. Philadelphia, PA: Griffing, Gordon and Company, 1889.

Bopp, Eddie. *Indianapolis Washington High School and the West Side*. Bloomington, IN: Author House, 2010.

Divita, James J. *Rejoice and Remember, 1891-1991*. Indianapolis: St. Anthony Parish Centennial Committee, 1992.

Divita, James J. Review of Etan Diamond, *Souls of the City: Religion and the Search for Community in Postwar America*. Bloomington: Indiana University Press, 2003.

Downey, Lawrence J. *A Live Thing in the Whole Town: The History of the Indianapolis-Marion County Public Library, 1873-1990*. Indianapolis: Guild Press of Indiana, 1991).

Dunn, Jacob Piatt. *History of Greater Indianapolis*, vol. 2. Chicago: Lewis Publishing Company, 1910.

Dunn, Jacob Piatt. *Indiana and Indianans: A History of Aboriginal and Territorial Indiana and the Century of Statehood, vol.2*. Chicago: The American Historical Society, 1919).

Durant, Samuel W. "Plan of Indianapolis" [map], in *Maps of Indiana Counties, 1876*, reprinted from *Illustrated Historical Atlas of the State of Indiana*. Chicago: Baskin, Forster & Company, 1876.

Greiff, Glory-June. "Public Schools and the Neighborhood Life-Cycle." Indianapolis: Historic Landmarks Foundation of Indiana, 1985.

Guthrie, Charles, Dan Briere, and Mary Moore. *Indianapolis Hispanic Community*. Indianapolis: University of Indianapolis Press, 1995.

Hale, Hester Anne. *Indianapolis: the First Century*. Indianapolis: Marion County-Indianapolis Historical Society, 1987.

Hurtado, A., S. A. Roberson, and Jan Shipps, "Stringtown Survey Report." *Indiana Historical Sites & Structures Inventory*. Indianapolis: Center for American Studies, 1985.

Holma, Marc E. "Reading, Writing, and Relinguish: The Abandonment of Historic Indianapolis Schools, 1970 to 1979" Master of Science Thesis, Ball State University, 1998.

Jackson, Kenneth T. *The Ku Klux Klan in the City, 1915-1930*. New York: Oxford University Press, 1967.

Julian, Cloyd. *My Story*. Greenfield, Indiana: Mitchell-Fleming Printing, 2002.

Leary, Edward A. *Indianapolis: A Pictorial History*. Virginia Beach, Va.: The Donning Company, 1980.

Madison, James H. *The Indiana Way: A State History*. Bloomington: Indiana University Press and Indiana Historical Society, 1986.

Moore, Leonard J. *Citizen Klansmen, the Ku Klux Klan in Indiana, 1921-1928*. Chapel Hill: University of North Carolina Press, 1991.

Nolan, Jannette Covert. *Hoosier City: The Story of Indianapolis*. New York: Julian Messner, 1943.

Polis Center. Indiana University Purdue University Indianapolis. *Study Neighborhoods*: "Near Westside." http://polis.iupui.edu/about/community/culture/project-on-religion-culture/study-neighborhoods/?neighborhood=near-westside

Entries from the Encyclopedia of Indianapolis

Bodenhamer, David J. and Robert G. Barrows, eds. *Encyclopedia of Indianapolis*. Bloomington, IN: Indiana University Press, 1994.

> Briere, Dan and Charles Guthrie and Mary Moore, "Hispanics," 683-85.
> Crumrin, Timothy. "World War II." 1463-65.
> Cynthyia Clendenon. "Flooding and Flood Control." 582.
> Divita, James J. "Demography and Ethnicity." 56.
> Donnelly, Cathleen F. "Kingan and Company." 870-71.
> Donnelly, Cathleen F. "Stringtown." 1306.
> Hale, Michelle. "School Segregation Case (U.S. v. Board of School Commissioners)." 1222-23.
> Hulse, Monte. "Overview: Neighborhoods and Communities." 135.
> Markisohn, Deborah. "Link-Belt Company." 919.
> Ogden, R. Dale. "Basketball." 307.
> Schneider, Mark E. "World War I." 1460-62.
> Shipps, Jan. "Religion." 180.
> Zeigle, Connie J. and Thomas Keiser. "Vietnam War." 1383-85

Unpublished Histories

Ollie Baus, "History of Mt. Jackson Cemetery" (paper presented at the meeting of the Wayne Township Historical Society, Indianapolis, IN, May 1, 1967).

Hazel Corwin. "A Brief Summary from the Historical Record of George Washington High School, 2215 W. Washington Street, Indianapolis, Indiana, 1927-1985" (paper presented to the Wayne Township Historical Society, Indianapolis, 1985).

"History of School 50," a typescript compiled by the staff of Nathaniel Hawthorne School, 75 North Belleview Place, Indianapolis, Indiana, 1953.